WORKBOOK PRESS LLC
187 E Warm Springs Rd,
Suite B285 Las Vegas NV 89119 USA

Website: https://workbookpress.com/
Hotline: 1-888-818-4856
Email: admin@workbookpress.com

Ordering Information:

Quantity sales. Special discounts are available on quantity purchases by corporations, associations, and others. For details, contact the publisher at the address above.

Library of Congress Control Number:

ISBN-13:   978-1-961845-55-8   Paperback Version
             978-1-961845-92-3   Digital Version

REV. DATE: 07/17/2024

FROM BOYS TO MEN

What a Support Soldier Endured in Vietnam

Written by: David Schimpf

Illustrated by: Joey Schimpf

TABLE OF CONTENTS

INTRODUCTION

A true story of what a typical support soldier endured in Vietnam. Most military personnel in Vietnam were not in direct combat but served as support troops. This is what I did, but it wasn't boring, far from it. You will find that out.

I served on an LCM, which is a Landing Craft Marine boat, similar to those who landed at Normandy in WWII. Although I was in the Army, the Army operated medium boat companies in Vietnam. Although our main job was to keep the military supplied with ammunition, C-rations, weapons, etc., we also went on missions up the coast to deliver tanks and ammunition. These missions were scary to say the least.

You will find humorous, strange, and uncommon occurrences that happened during the year I served. Some are combat related.

ABOUT THE AUTHOR

David Schimpf currently lives in Saginaw, Michigan, and has been married to Linda Schimpf for 55 years. We have two wonderful children, Joseph, living in Saginaw, and Angela Matthis, married living in Washington, Connecticut. We also have three grandchildren, Joe Schimpf, Freddie Matthis, and Eva Matthis.

David was born on May 26, 1946, to Fred and Eva Schimpf, German/Russian immigrants from Oberdorf, Russia. He graduated from Arthur Hill High School in Saginaw and also attended Kettering University. He began to umpire softball in 1984 and is still involved by serving on the USA Softball of Michigan state umpire staff at the current time. He retired from GM/Delphi steering systems as a prototype coordinator in 1999.

FOREWORD

If you are looking for a war story filled with lots of combat action, violence, or vulgar language, then this may not be the book for you. However, if you want to experience what it was like to spend a year in Vietnam for an ordinary soldier, then this is the book for you. This war story is just about an ordinary soldier enduring a tour of duty in Vietnam. There is a little action, and some great stories for you to enjoy.

I was drafted into the Army on December 15, 1965, during the big buildup of the military. Most of the soldiers in Vietnam or any war are support troops. That translates easily: They may have worked in supply, clerical work, engineering, drove trucks or jeeps, or hauled troops to destinations. My MOS was 61C20, a marine engineer. I served on a landing craft boat, similar to the ones who landed on the beach during Normandy, during WWII. These boats were larger than the Higgins boats during that time and were called LCM's, (Landing Craft Marine).

I was assigned to the Landing Craft Boat Company, the 1098th Transportation Corp in Qui Nhon. You may be wondering why was a soldier in the Army serving on a boat? The Army, not the navy, actually operated landing craft in Vietnam. This was one of the fairly large bases located on the central coast. Our company consisted of many tents, called hootches, which housed 10-12 men per tent. It was situated beside the airfield.

Again, we saw little action, but were involved in numerous missions up the coast to deliver tanks, ammunition, weapons, and supplies. We worked very long hours each day. This story will attempt to explain what it was like for a G.I. serving in this capacity.

It's been 50 plus years since that tour of duty and my memory isn't as good as it once was, but I relied on a couple of my Army buddies that I am still in touch with, Bryson McGill and Jerry Arnett, for some minor details. One never forgets the actual experience of being "in-country". Thank goodness I also had a polaroid camera to physically record many places on film, a tape recorder which I used to send tapes back and forth to home, and the letters I wrote. The tapes were especially helpful with the memory.

As I look back now, I wish I could have kept a diary, that would have been so helpful. I hope as you read this you will find it enlightening and give you a glimpse of what it was like for an ordinary GI in Vietnam.

If you have been there and experienced Vietnam, this should shake the memory tree. It did mine. Just sit back and enjoy.

PROLOGUE

The Vietnam War should have never happened, but it did, and it is a scar which will forever fester in American history. It was a war the politicians and the pentagon wanted and needed for their own materialistic, ideological and selfish reasons. Unlike WWII, Vietnam never seemed to have a real game plan to come to a justified end. We fought a defensive battle most of the time, which any military genius knows can't be won.

It didn't help any when the media and public turned against the war in the late 60's. This was the first "television war" and America could witness it firsthand in their living rooms. Seeing body bags, violence and actual battle is never good.

No skirmish, no battle, and certainly no war can ever be won with a strict defensive mode. It seems this was the scene of nature during the 60's and early 70's. Yes, there were some bombing and offensive battles, but for the most part, it was defensive. Whenever the United States military would go on the offensive we would usually regress back to the ways of a turtle, that is, pull our body and legs back into a shell and hope the aggressor would disappear. Please don't get me wrong, I am very pro- military and very patriotic. I am not anti-America. This war was just an atrocity from the beginning.

It also didn't help that the South Vietnamese army didn't have the heart to fight for its own freedom. A lot of time and effort was spent by our military to arm and train these men who would often cut and run. It took years before they became a true fighting army.

The United States military brass underestimated the will of the enemy. We tried to fight a conventional war against guerrilla style warfare. It was similar to what the British did when they fought the Revolutionary War, they thought every enemy would just line up and fight. Tanks for instance were just about useless in the dense jungle and rice paddies. The Viet Cong and North Vietnamese Army (NVA) had a great system to keep their forces supplied. They had the Ho Chi Minh trail in Cambodia and their immense tunnel networks.

Whenever the Ho Chi Minh was blown up by our air force, within a few days or sometimes hours, it was up and running again.

There just was no way the greatest military in the world with its tremendous power and force, modern technology, and superior weaponry, could lose a war on a stage not much larger than the state of California. That's a correct statement providing the war is staged to the point of trying to win! Vietnam was not the case. For one thing, America was not prepared. Many times, the enemy could not be distinguished from the civilians. The American soldier stood out like giant redwood trees in a forest of pine trees.

Just picture the war in reverse. Let's just say for arguments sake that the United States decides to fight a war with Canada and China takes sides with Canada. Could they distinguish a Canadian from an American if dressed alike? No. Now throw in the Chinese army fighting a defensive battle under those conditions. Get the picture.

But the worst thing the Pentagon and Washington allowed to happen was to not prepare the American fighting man for such a war. Extreme heat, humidity, and jungle was to face us and many a man was trained in the wintertime in the snow. Actually, using the term "man" to describe the average soldier in Vietnam would be a total falsehood. Most of the fighting "boy" was about 18-20 years old and many just out of high school. Considered too young to vote, too young to drink, and too young to purchase on credit, but old enough to kill, determine who the true enemy is, and handle oneself in a strange land and culture.

If the boy had the means to escape the draft and his parents had the wealth or influence, then he could just go to college and his worries were over for years. If he got married, he could escape the war during the early years, until that stipulation would change as the war dragged on and more "bodies" were needed. That left the poor, middle-class, or the uneducated to fight a war halfway around the world. Also, this would be the first year where young black men would be needed in great amounts. Thousands of our young men had never ventured more than a few hundred miles from home. Quite a shock to them to overcome.

Perhaps that was what Washington wanted. Place young men overseas, who won't ask questions or demand answers, won't defy authority, go forth in reckless abandon with no regard for their own lives and really have no fear, placing their own lives in jeopardy for the sake of "keeping communism over there."

It might have worked, but it seems like the war dragged on and the college kids knew they were going to be going to war also, began to protest. Most came from affluent families, and they felt the rug was being pulled out from under them. This is when the protest really took hold. If any one thing brought an end to the war it was the constant protests, flag burning, draft card burning, marches, etc. which really woke America up. The killing of students at Kent University in Ohio was the true tipping point. Shouts of "America, Get Out" resounded across the land. Walter Cronkite, the iconic news journalist saying on national television that we were losing the war was also a crushing blow.

Reflecting back on my own life, one which I feel was a typical Mid-Western American boy in the 60's. I was born and raised in Saginaw, Michigan, a mid-sized city of just under 100,000 of various races. In fact, I grew up on Maine street (almost Main street, USA). After graduating from Arthur Hill high school in 1964, I went to work for a General Motors parts plant. At the age of 19, I was sent a draft notice in October of 1965. My world was crashing down; I had a great paying job, a fast car (1965 Chevy SS), had a girlfriend and hung out with my guy friends. Like I said, typical middle class. Mature? Hardly.

I didn't know much about guns, having never shot anything more powerful than a BB gun. I knew very little about Vietnam or what was going on over there. My father, Fred, also worked for General Motors in a foundry. He was near retirement. My mother, Eva, was also a typical mid-western housewife. It seems like she was always cooking, cleaning or gardening. They were immigrants from Russia, Volga Germans, who came over on a ship as young children with their parents in 1912. I was brought up in a very strict but loving Christian home where you went to church every Sunday, read the Bible and prayed at night, respected the elderly, honored the flag, the country, and you didn't defy authority.

My brother, Don, was 10 years older than me and worked in the same General Motors complex as myself. Was married to Barbara Jo, and had four children, Michael, Cathy, Holly and Scott. Barbara Ann, my sister, was going through a rough marriage at the time and had three children, Kimberly, Wendy and Timothy. They were living in the basement of our modest, two-storey home at the time. That was my family and I loved them all.

Now back to my story. Remember I got drafted and was not very happy but awaited further instructions.

Photo of me with Mom and Dad

This book is dedicated to my mother, who was always an inspiration to me. Because my dad worked third shift and slept during the daytime, mom was my "rock". She was strict but kind. The most loving woman I ever knew. She got me through some tough times in my life and I was never able to tell her how much I appreciated her. She told me to look at the brightest star in the sky at night and talk to her. This I did just about every night in Vietnam.

I also want to dedicate this book to my many friends I made in Vietnam. Many I never saw or communicated with again. This leaves a void in my life. I miss you all and will never forget your faces.

Photo of my Mother and I
After returning home from Vietnam

CHAPTER ONE

RECEPTION STATION, FORT KNOX

I got a letter from selective services to report to the greyhound bus station to go to Fort Wayne in Detroit for physical examination. A few of my high school friends were on that bus as well. Going through the medical exam was very strange, as we had to strip down to just our underwear and walk single file from station to station. There were many other young men there from other cities. One time we were on an outside balcony which faced the street. When the examination was close to ending everyone was in a long line as men in charge were selecting guys to go to each branch of service. It was like; "army, army, navy, marines, etc." Guys were counting back trying to figure out what branch they could be in and wanting to switch spots so they wouldn't be in the marines. It was comical and scary. Lucky for me, I was selected for the army.

A few weeks later I received a letter stating I was to report for duty at Fort Knox, Kentucky on December 15, 1965. It was a sad day indeed saying goodbye to all my family. As I was waiting for the bus to arrive, a man from the Salvation Army was handing out small New Testament Bibles to each enlistee. The pastor of my church already had presented me with a Bible to read while in the army, but I took the small Bible anyway.

We arrived at Fort Knox that evening and as we were stepping off the bus, a drill sergeant began yelling at us to fall in. Nobody knew what to do, but he kept yelling and giving us instructions on what to do. After a few moments we were forming up in lines about 5 deep and he was using his loud deep voice giving us more instruction as to what we were to do. We were told we were at the reception station where we would be for a few days until assigned to an actual platoon. We were then led into a building where we were told to empty our pockets. Three men confiscated anything they deemed not needed. Pocket knives, combs, etc. were taken and never seen again. What was truly sad was that many had photos of girlfriends or wives which were taken. No reason was given but we wondered what those men did with those photos. It was well past midnight when we finally got to our large two-story wooden barracks to go to bed.

BANG, BANG, BANG! It was 5 a.m. and we were woken up by a drill sergeant beating on a large empty metal garbage can. Not what any of us was expecting. More yelling and screaming ensued as we were told to hurry up and get dressed for chow. We all fell out to a long line, got our metal trays and utensils, eggs and some kind of meat was dumped on our trays, and we sat and ate. Another drill sergeant was yelling at us not to talk, just eat quickly and take your trays over to be cleaned off.

There were three metal garbage cans filled with water at different temperatures. One garbage can had extremely hot water, then another with hot water and finally the third with lukewarm water. You had to dip each tray in each can until clean then place on a stack. The guy in front of me was told by some guy in a green fatigue uniform to take the stack of trays to a tent. I never saw that guy again, and quickly figured out he ended up on KP duty. As the day went on a few of us talked about this and I knew I didn't want to end up on KP duty. We also found out those guys in plain fatigues were just like us, new recruits with no real status to give orders.

After breakfast we were sent to a building to get our uniforms and gear. Being fitted for uniforms and boots was a joke. Everything was hurried up, measuring tapes were used, fatigues thrown at you, then to a seat to quickly try on two pairs of boots. Within an hour everything we needed was supplied, enough for about a week along with a large duffle bag to stuff it all into. Then it was off to the barber shop to get the GI haircut. I already had a short haircut, so it didn't bother me so much to have it all taken off, but some guys had long locks and watching them was actually humorous. Within about 5 minutes every hair was gone except for stubble on top. One thing a new recruit found out early was the army wanted everyone to look the same.

Now it was lunch time, and the same exact thing was being repeated. Eat fast, shut up, more yelling, and wash your tray. This time I was picked to pick up the stack of trays to take into the tent. I looked at the recruit, smiled, and I turned 1and ran away. He yelled but it did no good. I knew he was no different than me. He just selected the next guy in line to do the dirty work. When I told the story later that night everyone got a good laugh out of it.

Day two was more of the same, getting startled out of bed with a garbage can being beat on, breakfast, and now for some kind of aptitude testing. We were all taken to a large building with tables and chairs where instructors gave us forms to fill out. I recalled what my brother-in-law, Ron Suppes told me. He served as an MP in the army, and said when I take this test, don't blow it off, do the best you can. Those who don't do as well end up in the infantry. Now I was a fairly intelligent person, and I did my best which must have helped as I didn't end up as a "grunt" as those in the infantry were affectionately called.

Another form given to us had questions asking about our family, heritage, and other personal items. One question asked where each parent was born. My parents being immigrants, were born in Oberdorf, Russia. When my form was read, I was taken to another room for questioning. I remember what happened to this day. A man with some kind of rank sat across from me and asked me what I was up to. I stared blankly, and being slightly scared, asked him what he meant. He looked at me coldly and shoved the form I filled out back at me and said, "If you think saying your parents are Russian will get you out of the army, you are sadly mistaken." I told him, "I'm not trying to get out of anything, it's where they were born." I then explained the situation which then led to him handing me another form to fill out. This contained many questions about things concerning communism and the communist party. A few were: Did I belong to the Communist Party? Did I belong to the John Birch Society? After I checked all the boxes No, I handed it back, he appeared satisfied but unhappy. I was then told to leave the room. The interrogation was over.

After lunch we were all taken to a medical type of facility for examination and for our immunization shots. The examination was your basic one, stand there with just your underwear on, cough, breathe deeply, while vitals are checked. There were forms to fill out as to health condition. During my senior year in high school, I suffered two separate episodes of a collapsed lung. I was hospitalized both times. This I put down as well as the normal operations; appendicitis and tonsils removed.

I should mention that I was fairly healthy but very tall and slim. I was 6'4" and about 160 pounds.

After the physical exam, I got into another line for the shots. This was done with a device like a gun which would be pressed against your shoulder, one on each side, four total, and injected. Having been in the hospital a few times, getting shots never bothered me. Not so lucky for some of the other guys. Many stumbled outside and got sick or passed out.

Over the next few days there was less and less to do as we awaited our orders as to where we were to go next. We were all getting anxious, and many were calling home letting parents and friends know their status. We couldn't get any mail because we had no home base, it was necessary to let everyone know what was going on.

Finally, we were told that because Christmas is coming soon, they didn't want to assign us and then have nothing to do. It was decided that everyone could go home on a short leave and then return to their new assignments. Everyone was very happy about that. The problem for many who lived a long distance away was there were no planes available at such a short notice, so in order for those soldiers to go home, they would have to fly standby. The phones were jammed with soldiers trying to make some kind of arrangements. I decided the best way home was by bus, and they were getting on short supply also. I was able to book one called "express", which was a joke. Apparently express means it would stop at every major bus station.

What should have been about a 10-hour ride turned into a 14-hour ride home. Now for a little humor. When I finally arrived, my father was there to pick me up. I was one of the last ones off the bus and dressed in my dress uniform. My father walked up to me with a puzzled look on his face and asked me, "Are there any other soldiers on the bus?" I knew then that he didn't recognize me. I said, "Dad, its me." He smiled brightly and gave me a hug. I guess with my short hair, uniform and darkness, I didn't look the same.

Because Christmas fell on a Saturday in 1965, we were allowed until January 3rd to get back. The leaves were short but sweet and seemed to fly by. It was back on the bus and returning to Fort Knox for Basic Training to begin. Needless to say, my apprehension was getting the best of me as my next "chapter" in the army was about to begin.

CHAPTER TWO

BASIC TRAINING

Now the real training will begin. As most of the guys were gathering about a drill sergeant showed up. He was short in stature and was very military-like. He looked us over and then started in, "Hello girls, my name is Sergeant Jones, and I am your new mother." We now belonged to him for the next eight weeks.

Sergeant Jones then began his long, boisterous, obscenity laced speech. Whenever something occurred that would upset him, he would strut up, get into the soldiers' face and rip into him with an obscenity tirade which sometimes would be interrupted by him ordering a soldier to "Give me 20!" That was an order to get down and do 20 pushups. After a few of these incidents, we all caught on quickly to the fact that he meant business and he was in charge.

We now were ordered to pick up our duffle bags and double time to our new barracks. Forming two lines and shouting a cadence, we now ran down a street to our new home, a wood sided WWII style two storied building. Once inside we were grabbing whatever bunks were available. Unfortunately for me, I had the lower bunk next to the door, I would be the first one to be woken up by the incessant beating of a garbage can or a wall with a club by sergeant Jones. In the upper bunk was a classmate and friend from work, Dennis Druelle. In the next bunk was another work mate, Ed Magnus. They were the only ones from Saginaw that I knew as my other friends were assigned to different platoons or forts.

It didn't take long to figure out the makeup nationally of our platoon. It was basically half Michigan and half West Virginia. Of course there were the different races, but the chanting that would happen from time to time was pretty humorous. On one side of the barracks on the lower level was the guys from West Virginia and in their drawl, they would say they were from "West By God Virginia". That would be followed by the Michigan side, we are from "God's Country, Michigan". This good-natured bantering would continue for the entire 6 weeks together. It could start spontaneously in the middle of the day by someone and be answered. We became one group of soldiers thanks to that, and friends quickly became friends.

Each person had a footlocker and an upright locker. We were instructed as to the proper way to place clothes in the upright lockers in a very regimented order. In the footlocker, the green socks were rolled a certain way and along with underwear, placed in the bottom. On the top shelf was your shaving kit, toothbrush, toothpaste and other necessary items. Everything had to be very orderly and placed just so. Boots and dress shoes were placed under one side of the bunk. A white dot was painted on the heel of one pair of boots, they were to be worn on odd number days. This was done so you always had to polish them and also so the sergeant could tell you weren't trying to trick him, God forbid. Inspection could occur at any time and your items had better be in the correct order. Many a footlocker was dumped upside down by sergeant Jones when he saw otherwise.

Somehow, we found out that Sergeant Jones served two tours in Vietnam and saw combat. He was attempting to prepare each and every one of us for war if we ended up there. He was tough on all of us, and he was hated by many, but we still understood. One Sunday, which was usually our day off, we were ordered to clean the barracks and it was going to get the "white glove treatment". We knew that meant it had to be super clean. We worked all day and thought we had it made. In came sergeant Jones, and he was wearing white gloves. He walked around staring at everything without showing any emotion. Then he pulled over a footlocker, stood on it, and wiped his gloved hand across a beam, looked at it, jumped down and stood there. Now we were all lined up in front of our bunk beds and you could hear a pin drop. Then he held his hand up and showed his dirty glove. Need I say more? We spent the rest of the day and night thoroughly cleaning the barracks. Sergeant Jones never came back to inspect. He didn't have to, he knew. Lesson learned.

I would be remiss if I didn't mention that we were taking basic training in the middle of winter in Kentucky. Winters in Kentucky can be bad, but normally not near as bad as the ones in Michigan. Not this year. We went through some of the worst cold weather in the history of the state. The windowpanes on the inside had about a ¼ inch of ice on them nearly every morning. A couple days the butt cans froze over. Now butt cans are actually coffee cans hung on the upright poles in the middle of the barracks and half filled with water. Smokers would use them after the cigarettes were extinguished. It was determined that it was too cold to go outside for PT (physical training), so it was done in the barracks. This lasted two full weeks.

It wasn't just the weather that kept us confined. One of the soldiers in another barracks nearby came down with spinal meningitis. This is an acute inflammation of the brain and spinal cord and considered highly contagious in 1966. Because of this belief we were once again doing PT for an entire week in the barracks. So out of eight weeks of basic training, three were completed completely inside. This is almost unheard of.

Once we were finally able to be outside and do PT and running, we had a lot of catching up to do. Most marching and running was done over 5 miles. On one instance, I suffered some breathing problems, probably due to my lung conditions in the past. I couldn't finish and sat down on a stump. Sergeant Jones stood before me, and he was irate. He demanded I get up and cussed me out. After getting to my feet, he took my rifle and slammed it into my chest demanding that I continue. This did me in and I fell backwards and had to be taken to the hospital by jeep. This incident made sergeant Jones very leery of me and he had much disdain towards me, which was evident. Apparently, he thought I was faking it, as I had been cleared the next day from the hospital with no symptoms. Needless to say, I had to do numerous pushups whenever he felt it necessary. He was making an example of me.

My friend from Kentucky, Jerry Arnett, was another soldier sergeant Jones disliked. Jerry was severely overweight and sergeant Jones was determined that he was going to lose enough weight so he could pass basic training. Jones was relentless in the amount of exercise Jerry had to do to accomplish this. Jerry some how was able to get his weight down and graduate. Oddly enough, Jerry and I went through the entire two years of our service together. Yes, basic training, advance individual training (AIT) and Vietnam. We are still friends today and we get together about every other year.

One day we had to take rifle training and we marched to the rifle range for this. Large targets were set up in rows about 100 yards away. Back then, when you missed your target, a person would wave a pole with a red flag on it called "Maggie's drawers". These soldiers waving the flag were stationed in a trench directly below and to the side of each target. The term is believed to derive from a song in 1926 that soldiers sang, "Those little red drawers that my Maggie wore". I was far from an expert but did pass as a marksman.

The next day we went for grenade training. First, we were given dummy grenades, and shown how to throw them. There were about 6 bunkers set up and a soldier would go in with a ranked soldier who would hand you a live grenade. Now, if you have ever seen a movie where a soldier is shown pulling the pin of a grenade with his teeth, don't believe it. This pin is not easy to pull out, you hold the lever down and then throw it as far as you can. God help you if you drop it.

With about a week to go before we were done, we had to go through the obstacle course at night. Of course, the weather didn't cooperate as this was accomplished during a driving rainstorm which began early in the day. The only good thing, we didn't have to march there, we were driven there in trucks called "Deuce and a Halves" because they weighed 2 ½ tons. The course had been turned into a muddy, watery mess. Soldiers manned machine guns on stands on one end, and although they were shooting about 8 feet above us, it seemed like only a couple feet. We were instructed to carry our rifles and crawl through the entire course, under barbed wire at times, where you were to turn over on your back, place your rifle on your chest so it would get wet, and crawl work your way under the barbed wire. One time my head went under the water, and I had to hold my breath in order to get under and through. We were like drowned rats once we got back to the barracks. However, the night was not over, as after we all showered our rifles had to be thoroughly cleaned.

Private Todd and I in front of
gun rack Fort Knox

My footlocker in basic training
with rolled up socks

With just a few days remaining our platoon was to serve on nightly guard duty. The company commander, a captain, was the guard inspector and he would be driven around that night by a driver selected during the day who could best recite the chain of command and/or the general orders. This was the job everyone wanted because you didn't have to stand guard, you slept in a bed until the captain needed you to drive him. There were about 10 general orders to memorize, and the many chains of command ranks also, not an easy task. The captain would go down each line with sergeant Jones at his side, stand before anyone he chose, stare at the soldier and ask them a question or two. You then would have to answer like this as an example: "Sir, my 6th general order is…." Try not to blink, forget words or look away or it will be over. Guess who was selected to be the driver? Yep, none other than private Schimpf after I studied all day. I nailed all three questions thrown at me and sergeant Jones wasn't happy. Remember, he didn't like me much. I never had to drive the captain, but I sure had a good night's sleep. The next day, sergeant Jones stood before me and said, "Schimpf, I don't know how you did it." I just smiled. Lucky for me he was in a good mood, or understood I proved him wrong, as he didn't make me do pushups.

There were many more stories about basic training, some funny, some strange and some that were pretty bad. However, this book is about Vietnam. but I would be remiss to not lead you into what it was like to be trained for the war. Just think about that for a moment and reflect on what I wrote. Most of us were going to Vietnam, that was a given, a place that is unbearably hot, humid, and mostly covered with rice paddies and jungle. Yet, we were trained in cold, snow, and mostly inside. Does that sound like a great way to prepare a soldier for what is ahead of him?

We heard words of "guerillas", which most of us could only relate that to an animal in a zoo, not someone who was trying to kill you. How the enemy would hide in tunnels, trees, or in civilian clothes. How do you determine who they are? How a child could not be trusted no matter what age. They were known to be booby trapped with explosives. What in the hell were we getting in to?

The day before graduation day, sergeant Jones gathered us all together on the first floor to receive our final orders on where our next duty would be. Of course, everyone was hoping it would be Germany or the states, or anywhere but Vietnam. We were told that about 80% of us were going to Vietnam in some capacity. The silence was deafening as our names and printed orders were called off and handed to us. Imagine my shock when I found out it would be Vietnam but not the infantry. I was going to an advanced individual school at Fort Eustis, Virginia as a marine engineer. A person can be depressed and elated at the same time, and that was me. I would say most were told, "infantry, Vietnam". Those faces would turn ashen white upon hearing those words. When the meeting was over, everyone dashed for the pay phones to call home. I hated to tell mom and dad my assignment because I knew it would be devastating to them. My mother had five brothers who served in WWII and all returned home, so she knew what that was like.

Graduation Day arrived and there was a ceremony with each platoon involved. My parents didn't come, so when it was over, I traveled by bus home. I had a short leave before flying to Fort Eustis. All the way there I kept wondering what a marine engineer would be doing, I just knew it was some kind of boat duty.

My locker in basic
training

Private Maxwell and I
having some fun

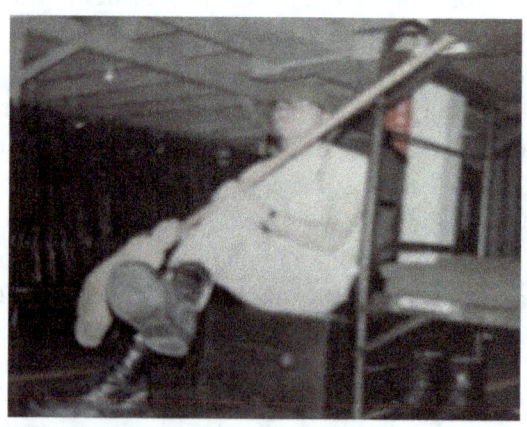

Private McNally having fun on
guard duty Fort Knox

CHAPTER THREE

A.I.T.

I took a cab from the airport in Richmond, Virginia to Fort Eustis. I was going to be there for another 8 weeks of Advanced Individual Training (AIT). What kind of training would that be? Who would I know? What kind of a boat would I be on? What does a marine engineer do? All of these questions and many more were going through my mind.

Upon arrival I had to report to the Company Commander of my new platoon. I was then taken to a very nice brick building which was a pleasant surprise. It had tile flooring, nice stairways and windows, but we still used bunk beds. I was almost expecting to see regular beds like in a motel. Some guys were already there for quite some time, but others were coming in and picking out beds, once again, I selected a lower bunk, footlocker and locker. I began putting my clothes and items away and making some new friends.

Then I noticed an old friend, Jerry Arnett. It was great to see him again. We were told to fall out for some orders and information. We all stood around as a sergeant told us what to expect. We would go to school in the morning after breakfast where we would be for the entire day. I wasn't used to the relaxed attitude of those with rank. Nobody yelling obscenities, screaming in your face, or ordering pushups, how strange.

The first day we were taken to the docks to see the different types of boats that were there. I was shown an LCM, which is a Landing Craft Mechanized. This boat has four diesel engines below deck, two on each side, called a bank of engines. Each engine is a straight line six cylinder with fuel injectors and a blower on top. We were given a quick tour of this boat and what it was capable of doing. An LCM is about 60 feet long and about 18 feet wide with a metal wheelhouse with throttles and a steering wheel.

In the afternoon we were taken to actual classroom settings where an instructor would explain what exactly a marine engineer's duty was on board.

We were told the coxswain was in charge of operating the boat while we were in charge of keeping it running. I doubt there were many in the room who knew much about diesel engines, myself included. Actually, when it came to diesel engines, I was clueless. This type of basic schooling continued for a couple of weeks, with some testing and great instruction.

Before long we were really getting into some hands-on work. The most complicated being the fuel injectors. A fuel injector has a cylinder inside which has tolerances so tight that a single fingerprint on it will make it almost impossible to re-assemble. Hard to believe, but true. We were all given one to use and then disassemble. We were told to grab the cylinder with two fingers and try to assemble it. Of course it didn't work, but it showed us exactly how we had to maintain cleanliness if we had to do this. I kept thinking that I hope I never have to do this.

We still had some barracks duty and kitchen police (KP), but it was rare. One day I was put in charge of three guys, mopping the two floors. I told them all we had to do was wet mop rather than strip and wax as the floors were in good shape. I left the two black's guys upstairs while I worked with another downstairs. After about an hour I went upstairs to see how they were doing, and I became irate. They ignored what I told them and started to strip the wax off. As I was chewing them out, I bent over to wring out the mop in the mop bucket on wheels. That was the last thing I remember coherently as I woke up in the hospital. Apparently, the guy in front of me either kneed me or he sucker punched me in the face. When I tried crawling to the steps I passed out. I was told when they found me the blood was flowing down the step and puddled there. My nose was badly broken, and I had two black eyes and suffered a concussion.

A buddy of mine who I got to know, Bryson McGill, visited me in the hospital and said I was almost unrecognizable. Because I actually didn't see how it Happened, when questioned about the incident, nothing was done about the two guys. Although I did remember who was upstairs, I told some guys what occurred when I returned to the barracks a couple days later. Now remember, this was Virginia and there were some good ole southern boys there who wanted revenge. I said it probably wasn't a good idea and to just let it go. Within a week those two black soldiers were transferred to another barracks.

We were allowed weekend passes and one time I went to Newport News, Virginia, which was a bust. Tons of GI's roaming the streets and not much to see or do. I made friends with Billy Campfield, who lived in Richmond, so one weekend I went there. I met a girl, his cousin, Lynda Bixler and we hit it off right away, we became pretty serious over the span of a couple weekends, and she promised to wait for me to get out. That put me on cloud nine. Now I also had a girlfriend back home, Yvonne Railling, and now I was wondering exactly how I was going to handle this.

We experienced a few more weeks of schooling with actual engines that were raised up above the floor so we could go up on a platform to work on them and also see from below. A diesel engine is pretty basic, so we were given just simple maintenance to perform.

Finally, our training was complete, and we awaited our final orders. We knew we were going to Vietnam but exactly where. Rumors were flying around that the boats were used for river patrol on the Saigon River, or there was many troop landings under heavy fire, or other dramatic ideas. This all proved to be false as the navy did the river patrol on PT like boats, and the troops basically arrived by plane or ship. We basically sat around for a couple of days just anxiously waiting and waiting.

Then we were given our orders. Qui Nhon was my destination with the 1098th Transportation Corp. This was all I would know. We were given a 14 day leave and to report to Fort Dix, New Jersey as we were flying to Vietnam. That sure was better than going by ship, which took about 20 days. Once again, the guys gathered around the two phone booths available to call home.

Because it was just before Memorial Day weekend, booking a flight was almost impossible. I didn't want to fly standby as I heard horror stories from some of the guys. So, I took a bus from Richmond, Virginia to Saginaw, Michigan.

Again, I was told it was an express Greyhound bus, which was another lie. The trip took about 18 hours.

Those two weeks flew by. It was now time to leave home, and it was truly sad to say goodbye.

4th student Company at Fort Eustis, Virginia

CHAPTER FOUR

GOODBYE AMERICA, HELLO VIETNAM

The flight from Fort Dix, New Jersey to Vietnam was a long one, over 20 Hours to completion. The night before was a restless one as many of us stayed up until the wee hours talking and wondering about what lay ahead for us. We were not all going to be in the same place or duty, so the talk all centered around each kind of duty we were getting into.

We boarded the Pan Am jet just as the sun was rising over the horizon. It was a solemn walk, many carrying little handbags, not knowing what to expect. Many of us I'm sure were wondering if we would ever see the good 'Ole USA again. I even wondered if I would return alive.

As we boarded the plane a pretty stewardess and the captain of the plane greeted us, with a quiet, "Welcome aboard". I quietly took my seat next to the window and listened as if a few were cracking jokes and were answering with half-hearted laughter. Quite a few were ogling the pretty stewardesses who really didn't look much older than most of us. I stared out the window and unfamiliar surroundings and reflected back on the last time I boarded a flight, it was the one which left Tri-City airport in Saginaw, for Fort Dix just a day earlier.

It was early evening and many friends and relatives along with family came to see me off. Of the many hugs and kisses, however, only one stuck with me. It was my mother's, as tears flowed down her cheeks and how sad she looked. As I started walking towards the plane, I turned to wave goodbye one last time and noticed my mother had left the crowd and followed me a little way and was standing by herself. I had to go back! No way could I leave her like that. I briskly strode up to her and hugged and kissed her one more time and tried to convince her not to worry, although she sobbed through those words. Again, I said everything was going to be OK, and I would write to her as much as possible. Although I didn't know what lie ahead, I knew I was coming back. I wonder how many GI's said or thought that and never returned.

I reluctantly boarded the plane and took a window seat facing the terminal so I could get one final glimpse of everyone who came to see me off. Tears welled up in my eyes as I realized this was the last time I would see them all for at least a year. Before long, the plane pulled away to taxi towards the runway, and I strained my neck and kept them in sight as long as possible. I looked at the surrounding homes and farmland until it was completely engulfed in darkness.

The sound of laughter and card games quickly snapped me back to reality. I was on a plane heading to Alaska to refuel and continue. Numerous poker games were going on all around me, many were going on since lift off. Seat backs were turned down into miniature tables and even some stewardesses joined in the play when asked or just watched. Of course, I had to join in a game as it was a long flight without much else to do, and besides I loved playing poker. Quite often a stewardess was asked to sit in on a hand for someone, but it was reluctant, because money was involved. They were assured it didn't matter, we just wanted them there. It turned into some of the longest games played as the flight took over 6 hours to Elmendorf, AFB in Alaska.

The game I was in was pretty good, 5 or 6 guys playing for nothing big but interesting. The stakes quickly went from nickel/dime to quarter/half to a dollar or two. I was fairly lucky and got some decent hands and won some decent money. I actually ended up winning what was believed to be a diamond ring from one GI who couldn't cover the pot. I had the ring for quite some time and never checked to see if it was real. The problem with the games was that it seemed most of the guys could care less if they won or lost. It was like where we are going, who cares, money doesn't matter anyway. Even the high stakes games were like that. Nobody got angry if they lost.

The only pause in the action was when the plane was flying over the Canadian rockies, and everyone wanted to take in the sight out of the tiny windows at the snow-covered majesty below. Later as the plane began to descend the card games had to come to an end and seats put back into place. The view of Alaska was absolutely spectacular.

Alaska in June is truly a beautiful setting. The snowcapped mountains all around were the most gorgeous I have ever witnessed or ever will see in my lifetime. However, the stopover was going to be short, just about an hour or so, long enough to refuel, and refill the galley. We were allowed to go into the terminal and have some snacks, drinks and stretch or legs. The terminal had large windows almost around the circumference, which allowed for an awesome view. As the mountains rose around us, the temperature was a very comfortable 60+ degrees. It sure was tough to re-board the plane for our next destination, Tokyo, Japan.

Now flying across the Pacific Ocean is one long, boring flight. Because we were basically racing the sun it was still light outside and nobody really felt like napping, although a few did. Once again, the card games broke out. I settled into the same seat as before and our game resumed. All around was laughter and sometimes a happy scream from a stewardess who would win a hand for a soldier.

I finally convinced a pretty little stewardess to sit down and play a couple of hands for me for luck. She sat on the arm of the chair but was reluctant to play for real money, but I reassured her it was OK. She didn't win any hands and of course, I could care less, and she apologized as she got up to leave. Again, I had to reassure her that it OK and I didn't mind. Before long we were nearing Tokyo and the games had to end.

As we flew in low over the sprawling city, we witnessed what was so beautiful from above, was truly not so now. There were many shacks jammed in together, many made of just cardboard or scrap wood. The lower we got the more the city divulged the impoverished huts of the massed and crowded poor.

Once on the ground, we were told we could not go into the terminal because the stop would be very short for refueling only. We were allowed to get off and mingle around the tarmac, look at the distant sights, and then re-board for the final leg of the flight. Next stop, Tan Son Nhut airport in Saigon, Vietnam.

We were told that the flight would only take a couple of hours and it wasn't long after takeoff that some card games broke out again. I decided to just look out the window and let my mind drift. It must have been the reality of where we were going as the games didn't have the same gaiety, and they broke up after about an hour. It got quite a bit quieter as the soldiers tried to catch a few Z's or were reflecting on anything of value, more than likely home and family.

What was truly eerie about the entire 20+ hours of the flight, few talked about home or to anyone they didn't know. It was a close-knit group and it remained that way. I don't remember anyone even asking anyone about home, family or girlfriends either.

As we neared land everyone now wanted to see what most certainly had to be Vietnam. Actually, the sight in the distance was quite breathtaking, as it looked really quite lovely and peaceful. Not at all what I was expecting to see. Rolling hills were everywhere and rivers and streams seemed to knife through the lush greenness of it all. It made for a pretty green/blue contrast.

As we got closer to what most certainly had to be Saigon, the Captain spoke over the intercom and told us to fasten our seat belts and prepare for a quick and possibly hard landing. No circling the runway was done as the landing had to be quick to avoid any possible potshots from any enemy which might be nearby. The jet swooped down from the sky and before I realized it, the runway was below, and we came in for the quickest, most abrupt landing I can remember.

As I inched forward towards the door at the front of the plane I will never forget the look on the stewardess's faces. They had tears in their eyes and one particular strawberry blonde, petite young stewardess said, "Good luck guys, we will be looking forward to flying your home again soon." I'm sure she knew as most of the crew did, that a lot of these guys would not be returning home except in a body bag.

As I got closer to the door, the bright light coming into the plane seemed as though someone was shining a searchlight inside. In just a few seconds I would get my first glimpse of my new "home". Vietnam was just outside waiting for me.

CHAPTER FIVE

DAY ONE IN HELL

The heat was unbelievable! It was like standing in front of a blast furnace! This was as close to hell as I ever wanted to be. Perhaps it was because of the air-conditioned cabin of the plane I just left that made it so unbearably hot and humid. No, this was the real thing. It had to be 120 degrees outside I thought. I wanted to turn around right there and get back on that plane and say, "Take me home!" Unfortunately, there was no round trip ticket in my hand.

As I walked down the stairs of the ramp, I looked around at the sight before me. What looked so beautiful just moments before from the air sure looked gray, dingy and horrible now. There was concrete everywhere and barbed wire surrounding everything. The terminal was a gray, cement building which didn't look too inviting as all of us hurried towards it.

Now it seemed hotter than ever, as the scorching heat seemed to rise right out of the concrete beneath us and envelop my body. Sweat was pouring out of my armpits, back, neck and face. Maybe it was fright, but it sure felt like hell itself slapping me in the face.

Once inside the terminal it seemed a little cooler, as large ceiling fans were whirling above trying weakly to cool off the inside. I sat my duffel bag down at my feet and took a leaning position against the wall with my arm extended. My palm was against the wall as I gazed all around. A quick skittering of something light across the back of my hand suddenly startled me.

I jerked my hand back quickly and spotted a small light-green lizard climbing up the wall right where my hand was. I retreated back a few steps, never having seen a lizard this close before, only to witness a sight that is etched in my memory to this day. It still gives me the creeps. There were bugs, spiders, and all species of creepy, crawling creature crawling all over the walls and in corners on the floor. It seemed like the entire wall was moving.

I just stood and slowly turned looking at all of the walls. Then I looked around me and noticed all of the Vietnamese people working in the terminal. They all looked a little creepy to me in their black "pajamas" and flip-flop sandals as they skittered about staring at all of us. I thought, "My, what a God forsaken place." Bugs, lizards, creepy little people all around me were giving me cold chills.

We were then told to form up outside and prepare to board a bus for the trip to the reception center, also known as Long Binh. This was located about 10-15 miles northeast of Saigon. The bus looked like a regular school bus from home, only it was blue and white and had Air Force written across the side. The big difference was the wire mesh screens rather than windows which gave it the appearance of a prison bus. We were told the screens were for our protection from possible projectiles or grenades being tossed in by "Charlie", the Viet Cong. As we drove by what seemed thousand s of people on the road, most looking alike, the thought of any of them throwing hand grenades at us, made my hair stand on end.

When you are green, scared, and it's your first day in country, I took all of it in and thought the worst. What truly struck me was how women and men would just urinate at the side of the road and little children were bare naked all over. What kind of place was this anyway? They just ignored us as we went by, probably because it happens so frequently.

We found out soon enough that we were going around Saigon not through it. I started to notice numerous street vendors on the three-wheel tricycles with large baskets and umbrellas on them selling everything from Coca Colas and beer to cigarettes. All US made products by the way. Some were selling raw fish, and meat hanging on hooks. I'm not sure what kind of meat it was as I doubt it was beef.

Once away from the city life, it didn't take long for the country to take over and rice paddies to show up everywhere and Vietnamese working in the fields. Women were everywhere carrying pails of water on each end of a wooden rod over their shoulders, or with baskets on their heads as they scurried on the side of the road. The women had large rim straw hats on to help keep the hot blazing sun off their pitch-black haired heads. Young women and old women all looked alike. Not one of them even bothered to lift their heads and look up as we drove by.

We finally turned onto a narrow, almost two-lane road and into the debarkation center. It reminded me more of a concentration camp. There was a ditch and concentina wire rolled up all around with guards everywhere, including two heavily armed guards at the large wooden entrance gates. There were all kinds of kids milling about just outside looking for handouts, mostly candy. When we finally stopped and got off, we put our duffel bags down and hardly anyone said a word. The reality of where we were had finally set in. June 21, 1966, was a day I will remember for the rest of my life.

Then my eyes were drawn to a large crater just a few yards away, then another and another, each filled with rainwater, which seemed to be almost boiling in the hot sun. I found out later that the evening before some incoming mortar or rocket fire hit the base and a few soldiers were injured, one killed. What was truly sad is that soldier was on his way home. His last day was also his last breath.

A GI told me not to worry about those craters, as the attacks happen quite frequently. He said, "You don't have to worry about the ones you hear, because they are going over your head, it's the ones you don't hear that kill you." We talked for a bit in our bunks, and I found out he was going home tomorrow. Here I was just getting here, and he already spent his time in hell and going home. I remember he looked about 30 years old, but he was only 21.

But I'm getting ahead of my story and my first day. We took our duffle bags and sat them on the sandy soil and piled our other belongings on top. We were then taken to the chow line and another incident took place which is sealed in my brain. We were given eggs (powdered eggs), cardboard like bacon, toast and what looked like a carton of real fresh milk. I looked at my tray and thought this can't be too bad, little did I know what would happen next. The eggs had no taste at all, and the bacon was now swimming in grease, but hunger fixed that. Then I opened the carton of milk and poured it into a plastic mug and large chunks and lumps plopped in. The smell of rotten milk and food in my stomach made me wretch and I barely made it to the barbed wire and threw up. I was very queasy the rest of the day.

After that meal we were in orientation most of the day, inside and outside tents. We were informed about the people and their culture, how to be constantly on guard as you may think they are friendly but the V.C. are everywhere. They said to be on special guard for innocent looking children as one of the favorites. The trick of the VC was to strap explosives to an unknowing child and have them walk up to GI's and blow everyone to bits. You were to trust no one, help no one, and especially don't give food to anyone.

We were told there was so much venereal disease that some didn't even have a name yet. A sergeant said, "If you get the clap, expect an Article 16 for it." They said how the whores would place cut glass in the bottom of the "Saigon Tea" (watered down booze) which would disable a GI. Many other horror stories were told for all of us to be wary of.

As we were in this large tent near the end of the day getting more information, it began to rumble with thunder outside and then the skies opened up and it poured. I never saw anything like that before, as it rained so hard you couldn't see across the wooden sidewalk to the other tent. Within 15 minutes it was over and then it really got hot and humid.

We were told to fall out and get our gear and head for our sleeping quarters. Do you remember where I said we placed our duffle bags and gear? You are right, it was still outside, and now my duffle bag was almost under water and little streamlets were finding their way through the sand making miniature rivers. I was more fortunate than others, who set their gear in holes, now totally covered in water. All of my fatigues were wet and damp and of course my socks were soaked. What a way to end the day.

Just picture me now. After a very long flight, my initiation to Vietnam was going to bed hungry, as I still couldn't eat again, damp, thoroughly exhausted and even my bunk was damp. After the aforementioned conversation with the GI going home, needless to say, I didn't sleep that well. I lay awake listening to far off rocket fire and explosives probably a few miles away. As I drifted off, I thought, "How am I going to survive this."

CHAPTER SIX

QUI NHON, VIETNAM

Day two dawne5321232d the next morning. After another hearty breakfast of powdered eggs and cardboard bacon sans the milk, as I was still squeamish from yesterday. Everyone now gathered outside a large canvas tent for our final destination orders.

A sergeant came out in jungle fatigue and standing on a wooden porch about a foot off the sand, gave a quick summation of what we heard the night before. This was more of a reminder than a warning this time. He added, don't trust the kids, they could be booby-trapped too. Finally, he began to shout out names and assignments. Everyone was stretching their necks in order to hear. Then I heard my name, "Private David Schimpf, 1098th Transportation Corp., Qui Nhon," It didn't mean much to me as I had no idea where Qui Nhon was, but I had an idea what the 1098th was, probably a medium boat company.

Immediately after hearing my assignments, I moved towards a large map which was displayed on the porch, looking to find my next home. I heard guys asking other guys where a certain place was as they couldn't find it. I found Qui Nhon on the map and could tell it was a fairly good size city on the central coast about halfway between Saigon and the DMZ (Demilitarized Zone). I was correct, the 1098th was a Landing craft, medium boat company.

Just about everyone who came over with me from Fort Eustis was boarding a C-130 transport plane for the flight to Qhi Nhon. Les Cimino was the only one from my school who went somewhere else, he ended up assigned to a BARC Company (A boat that could also go on land). A C-130 is a very large four-engine prop plane, heavily camouflaged with no windows. There were strap-basket like seats along each wall of the fuselage with everyone facing each other. It was very dim inside because of the lack of windows.

We were told the trip would only take about an hour and we would be flying at a fairly high altitude to avoid rocket fire and then we would swoop down and land on the runway to avoid small arms fire. Let me tell you, those words were pretty frightening to a green soldier.

The trip was a little rough and to say we "swooped in" would be a huge understatement. Not being able to see outside didn't help at all and it felt like we were going to dive a bomb right onto the runway. Landing on the metal plated (PSP) runway was extremely loud and different sounding than we expected which made it quite frightening. Then the pilot put the brakes on, the engines were thrust into reverse so we wouldn't crash into the mountains at the end of the runway. It felt like we were going to be thrown right through the bulkhead of the plane. I don't think I've been so happy to be on the ground before.

As we filed off the ramp on the end of the plane once again the heat and humidity were unbearable. Once on the tarmac I could feel a slight warm breeze coming from the South China Sea at the other end of the runway. The mid-day temperatures during the summer months ranged from the mid-90 to over 100 degrees.

There were hills and mountains surrounding about two-thirds of the airfield and they actually looked quite beautiful in the distance with lush, thick green foliage. They seemed much closer, like they sprouted right out of the side of the runway, and it felt like I could almost touch them. I could barely see palm trees swaying in the distance and the cool blue South China Sea was visible at the East end. I could have fooled you into the feeling of being on a tropical south Pacific Island.

Seeing the tents of an obvious military company on the other side of the runway and fairly large building in the distance snapped me back to reality. Little did I know but that tent "city" was actually my new home, the 1098th. I could have walked over there but we had to be transported.

The sound of helicopters broke the silence from time to time as they came in over the hills and landing about a mile away. An Khe, which was usually under attack was about 30 miles away to the west, and Pleiku, in the central highlands, about another 60 miles beyond that. Chances are they were bringing casualties to a large field hospital nearby. Those were two places we would frequently hear about.

Before long a deuce-and-a-half truck showed up which would take us to our new company. As we rode in the back of the open truck through the outskirts of town it seemed like a serious lack of protection as we passed Vietnamese on bicycles and walking. Any one of them could lob a grenade into the back of the truck and wipe out about 20 guys with no trouble at all. Very strange.

There was little cardboard and wooden shacks along both sides of the main road (actually highway 1). Some were made out of various cans that were squashed and nailed to wood panels. The South China Sea was on our right and could be seen in the distance at times with swimmers frolicking in the surf. It almost looked like a typical summer day in the states. However, the barbed wire, black pajama clad Vietnamese on both sides of the roads told me otherwise.

Once again, the people just seemed to ignore our truck as we kicked up dust passing them. Little alleyways could be spotted along the road where the Vietnamese were mingling about buying various products from roadside stands or tricycles. Others had wheelbarrow like carts with fruit, vegetables and rice for sale. Women were everywhere in flip flops carrying water over their shoulders.

The truck would kick up choking dust whenever it veered off the oil covered asphalt road and I found it amazing the people could even breathe on the side of the road when this happened. For my first view of Qui Nhon, it wasn't a pretty one. Tomorrow I will see more of the city.

I remember seeing little children everywhere. Toddlers and pre-teenagers scurrying about everywhere with no real direction. Most were shirtless with bunched up pants made to look like shorts. The really tiny ones, boys and girls were either naked or wore little t-shirts with their naked bottoms showing below. Amazingly enough they seemed very happy. Children are always clueless as to what their lives are really like or their surroundings. I noticed there were very few teenagers. They may have been working, helping at home, or perhaps drafted into the army, or worse yet, they ended up being VC.

One thing you never got out of your nostrils was the stench that seemed to be everywhere and on everything. Perhaps it was the dogs, or the cattle being

35

used, but it was probably the urine and fecal matter in the small ditches on each side of the road. It was a common occurrence to see a woman or man to just stop, roll up their pants and squat and go to the bathroom. No shame, no self-consciousness is just a part of everyday life. I forgot they have no running water, toilets, or bathrooms.

This is one thing I never got used to seeing as I can close my eyes and still vividly see it today. In fact, I know if I close my eyes and concentrate, I swear I can go back and smell Vietnam. It's a smell that is unforgettable.

Finally, the truck pulled into the military compound. As we piled off the truck, we got our first glimpse of our new company. We have arrived at the 1098th Transportation Company. There were hootches everywhere and all connected by wooden sidewalks slightly elevated over the searing hot sand so your feet wouldn't burn.

Once assembled at the rear of the truck, we awaited instructions from the customary greeter, the "1st Shirt" (sergeant major) and the C.O. (company commander) who was a captain. The 1st shirt was a tall, husky, John Wayne type who seemed pleasant enough but also intimidating to the point you knew you better not screw up so you wouldn't be called into his hootch. Although I don't remember everything, he told us, it was basic orientation on what to expect and do.

The captain stood about 6 foot tall and weighed about 190 pounds. Pretty lean and fit, just like one would imagine he would be. He probably came right out of West Point and was very businesslike. He greeted us, told us this was a support group which consisted of "Mike boats" short for medium landing craft. I explained what a landing craft was earlier. The loading area was called a well and was about 40 feet long and about 8 feet deep. A ramp was in the front operated by two cables on each side with a wheel to operate it.

When the captain was done, another GI with a specialist insignia on his arm gave us our hootch assignments and one by one we followed him to our new home.

Myself standing next to reject pole.
This is my favorite photo of me In Vietnam

Aerial photo of the 1098th And the airfield

Map of Qui Nhon

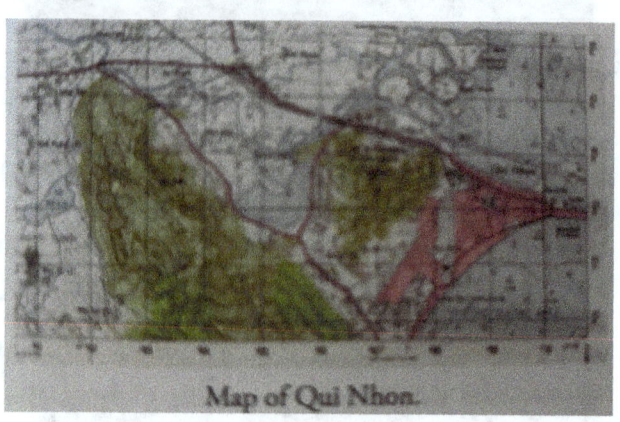

Map of Qui Nhon.

CHAPTER SEVEN

ARACHNOPHOBIA

Hootches were tent-like houses built on plywood sheets about a foot above the sand. The lower sides were about three-foot-high plywood with a canvas tent covering and a fine mosquito netting above the plywood walls. Each hootch was about 40-foot long and about 18 feet wide and big enough to accommodate 12 men, six on each side. On each end was a flap like canvas opening and three main support poles were located in the middle of the floor about 10 feet apart.

My area in the tent was in the middle and about 8 feet square. My narrow and short metal bed had a 4-inch mattress over springs stretched side to side. Not that comfortable but certainly better than many soldiers in the field. A mosquito net was draped over the bed by two T-shaped poles on each end for support. A hand -made wooden shelf from wooden crates was next to the bed and a long wooden shelf ran the entire length about 6 feet above the floor. A metal pole was attached end to end just below the shelf to hang your clothes on and your boots, shoes and flip flops were placed under the bed. My rifle was hung on two u-shaped hangers on the side of the bed. The wooden crates were used for towels, toiletries, and other necessities. On the side of the crate facing the bed usually a picture, fold out of a playmate, or some pretty movie star was taped. This was a reminder of the round-eyed American girls back home. All of the permanent items listed above were left there by a previous GI.

It took me a few weeks to accumulate all the items I would need to make the place as cozy as could be. At the PX (post exchange) I purchased some necessary items, and I bought a very colorful red wooden foot locker from Mama San in the nearby village. This was placed beside the bunk and contained valuables under lock and key. I bought a polaroid camera and a reel-to-reel tape recorder to use to send my voice back home and get one in return. Nothing of value was left unlocked, not because of the guys, but because each hootch had a Vietnamese house girl attached to keep it clean, polish our boots, and make our beds. The military hired them and others around the compound, so they had a paid job.

I taped photos of my favorite girls I knew from home under the lid (see photo), including my new girlfriend from Virginia, Lynda Bixler. We had a real thing going which came to a crushing end via a "dear John letter". But that's another story in another chapter. Of course, family photos were across the top, which was needed for that special incentive to return home. Every soldier in the hootch did about the same with their footlocker. Underwear, socks, and other clothes were stored below a wooden shelf in the footlocker. I would later make room for a cardboard cheese box where I would keep my letters from home. I still have it today, but it now contains those girl pictures and photos from Vietnam. Letters were so important to keep as I would re-read them from time-to-time.

It didn't take long to realize that clothes kept too long in the footlocker would become damp and musty. They were soon placed on the shelf. It also didn't take long to figure out that I needed to shake my clothes out before putting them on. Why is that?

Vietnam has to have the biggest cockroaches and spiders in the world! We had a nickname for the cock roaches, they were "super roaches", because they were just so huge and nearly indestructible. One could stomp on them numerous times with your boots on and then they would finally die. It had to be a super hard shell on their backs. If you didn't shake your clothes out before putting them on you might have one scrambling down your back or up your arm, or worse yet get into your pants. Believe me there isn't anything much worse than having a crawling critter in your shorts.

Another important detail I did was to fully inspect my pillow and bed before you crawled into it, in fact completely throw back the sheet. One night I was lying in bed reading by candlelight when I felt something crawling across my chest. I very carefully peeled back the sheet, not wanting to be frightened of whatever it was. "It" was the biggest, hairiest, bone-chilling ugliest spider God ever created. Now, mind you, I never was afraid of bugs or spiders in my life. We used to have a canned goods cellar in the basement and my mom and sister used to get me to bring up items because of the bugs and spiders down there. They never bothered me. They do now! Since my tour of duty in Vietnam, I cannot go near a spider, no matter how big. If I know one is in a room with me, I'm gone until its killed. It's called arachnophobia. It's amazing how a phobia happens.

Well, needless to say, I jumped out of my bed, and I proceeded to give that spider a quick brush of the hand to get him off my body. I then beat it to a bloody spot on the floor. I couldn't get a wink of sleep the rest of the night, as I kept staring at my surroundings wondering what else may crawl on me.

The very next night either he was resurrected from the dead or his father was out for revenge. When I turned back to sheet to inspect my bed, there he was, laying on my bed, and just as big if not bigger than the one I killed the night before. Once again, I beat this one to a bloody pulp which meant my sheet on my bed had to be cleaned the next day. I just went to bed on my bare thin mattress and tried to fall asleep.

Looking back at it now, it seemed to be a daily ritual in the hootch of stomping on super roaches or finding one of the creepy critters in their bed. Once in a while someone would yell out after stomping away, "I got one, I got one of the dirty sons-of-bitches."

This wasn't all we had to worry about, we also had several varieties of critters living beneath the hootch, from snakes, rats, and little green lizards. They usually didn't bother us too much because they liked dark, damp places rather than being messed with by us. "Leave well enough alone" is a good rule of thumb. The raised wooden floor was a haven for these critters.

The state of Texas does not hold a candle to growing things extra-large when you compare it to Vietnam. The rats were as big as tom cats, which might explain why we never saw any cats. Our compound had several dogs we called "ratters". They were mostly German shepherd mix, but they were the best ratters on the face of the earth. At least once a month, usually in the middle of the night, the chase was on. A rat would be racing through the tent with a dog, barking, close behind. The dogs were always treated with love and respect not just for the job they did, but also because it was a small reminder of home to have a dog.

One night in another hootch, the merry chase was on when a GI who was either high on pot or drunk decided to take matters in his own hands. He grabbed his rifle and began blindly shooting at the rat. He narrowly missed some of his mates and for this he was busted. For this crazy incident the whole company was basically punished. The C.O. ordered all weapons confiscated and placed in the arms room. This would result in a peculiar incident for me later, but that's in another chapter.

Speaking of smoking pot and drinking beer, that went on a lot too, although I never had the urge to smoke grass and neither did my close buddies I hung around with. Just about every day, in the back of the tent a small group of guys would hang out and light up a few. The smell at times would be so great the rest of us would go somewhere else, usually the "club" which was a hootch built just for hanging out and drinking beer. This was located about 100 yards next to the runway.

Our "bag" was to drink beer and lots of it. We usually went to the club to do this because the beer was cold and cheap. It was too difficult to have cold beer in our hootch. You could always tell when a shipment of beer arrived, because that would be the brand until another shipment came in. It didn't matter if it was Budweiser, Miller, Ballentine or some off the wall brand, as long as it was cold. If the club was too crowded to play poker, another of our favorite past times, we would buy some beer and take it back to the hootch.

We had the usual four or five poker players that were together also at Fort Eustis, myself, Bryson McGill, Jimmy Johnson, Billie Campfield and Hank.

Photo: poker game: L to R
Billie Campfield,Hank Hoefs,
Bryson McGill and Jimmy Johnson

Photo: Gary Pollock (L) and
Caleb Collins writing letters

Photo of myself outside
of the hootch

Me sitting on my footlocker in
my hootch writing letters

Hootch cleaning girl - Missy Lei

C-130 taking off from airfield

Hoeffs from Seattle. Once in a while someone else would sit in like Gary Pollock from Des Moines, Iowa or Caleb Collins, from Chicago. Out of our entire tour of duty the five of us might have missed playing poker about 30 days. That's a lot of cards playing, but it sure helped to pass the time.

Bryson McGill was from Woodruff; South Carolina and he would become one of my very close friends. He was married and expecting his first child. Also married were Hank Hoeffs and Jimmy Johnson from Richmond, Virginia. Billy Campfield and I were the only single regular card players. Gary Pollock and Caleb Collins were also single, but they actually didn't arrive in our hootch until late in the year.

Our game was mostly just nickel/dime just to keep it friendly and also because when you play that much, you need the money to last for the entire month.

We played in the club during the daytime and in the hootch at night under one of the three light bulbs that hung through the middle of the hootch. We would pick a footlocker for a table and sit on a bed on each side. The game was dealer's choice of five or seven card stud or three card draw. Although I never got a royal flush, I did hit a "double gut" straight flush. I had the 9, Jack, and King of spades and drew two cards, the 10 and Queen of spades. Very rare indeed.

Now to describe the compound, which consisted of about 15 hootches in Three rows of five each. Everything was connected by a slightly raised wooden sidewalk about 3 feet wide. The mess hall was the largest actual building and was situated the furthest from the runway and alongside that was the captain and first shirt's hootch. The arms room was next to their tent and then the little white camper trailer, about 8 feet long by 5 feet wide. which served as the "post office". There were no greater words than "mail call" and no greater disappointment than not getting anything from home. We also had a movie screen, which was a wooden wall that was used to protect the huge shower unit on a platform with a large water tower next to it.

Nobody had to worry about KP, as that was done by villagers who were also paid. However, there was one duty nobody wanted, and we wondered why the villagers weren't allowed to do. That was the nasty job of burning human waste. Yes, you read it correctly. There were two out houses built above ground near the runway and underneath were two 50-gallon drums cut in half to catch the waste. When the wind was blowing over the runway a couple of GIs would have to use a long pole to pull out each drum and pour gasoline on the waste and set it on fire. The stench in the air was horrendous and it's another smell that I can vividly recall when necessary. Naturally I had this duty a couple of times.

As for our "movie theatre", this was used once or twice a week and I would must take a crate to sit on. I remember two movies that I watched, "The Russians are Coming, The Russians are coming", a comedy set in New England and the tearjerker, "Born Free". I say tearjerker because there probably wasn't a dry eye from all of the rough and tough guys who watched Elsa the lion and her cub. I'm not sure why it was so popular, but it had the largest audience.

Like I said earlier, the shower was directly behind the movie screen for privacy. There was a long pipe coming from the water tower with about a dozen faucets attached. If you wanted a hot shower, you had better be one of the first to arrive while the pipe was still hot from the sun. You can almost visualize the sight of a truck emptying, the mad dash to your hootch, grab a towel and soap, and hurry to the shower to be one of the first.

Unfortunately, my hootch was one of the furthest from the shower. That meant it was also close to the perimeter, which consisted of a wall of sandbags about three feet high with concertina wire behind that. A guard tower was nearby and beyond the wire were the backyards of the small village. Sometimes we would watch the small children playing and some would try to get close and beg for items, like candy. We were not allowed to do this, but it never stopped them from trying. Perhaps they also wanted to see American soldiers. The 1098th even had a barber. He was a villager who would not only cut your hair, trim a mustache, nose and ear hair, clean your ears and even gently crack the bones in your neck with the greatest technique. The cost: just 25 cents. That's the story of our home away from home, the 1098th.

Jimmy Johnson, Billy Campfield,
and I having fun

Bryson McGill and Jerry Arnett
helping Billy Campfield

Me in front of Foxtrot
23 Wheel House

CHAPTER EIGHT

90 HOUR WORK WEEK

The average work week for the 1098th was 90 hours! Yes, you read that correctly, 90 hours. I worked 12 hours each day, six days a week, and on Sunday, I worked 18 hours straight to shift changeover from either day to nights, or vice versa.

The day shift began at 6:00 a.m. and ended at 6:00 p.m. each day and on Sunday the day began at 6:00 a.m. and ended at midnight. This would allow for the shift to change to nights the following week. The only good thing about this was you had 18 hours off before that shift started. Whoopee! The night shift began on Monday at 6:00 p.m. and ended at 6:00 a.m. and continued until Sunday when it would end at noon. This of course would flip flop back and forth every week. Switching back and forth every week was a real drag. Your mental clock just couldn't get used to it. The only days off were Christmas and Thanksgiving when we got to eat a great meal at the compound.

Working nights on the boat wasn't too bad because it meant I could catch an hour or two of nap time if you weren't really busy. One of us would stay awake and keep watch while the other slept, which wasn't easy as there was no bed on board.

Usually, it meant laying down on the deck and using a couple life jackets for pillows. It was particularly easy if our boat was tied up with others in the inner harbor or tied up on the canned docks. It was called this because it was manufactured out of hundreds of empty 55-gallon drums underneath a metal platform extended out to the beach. If you were extremely lucky and got a load of broken wooden pallets or cardboard, you could be tied up for days to unload as this was the lowest priority.

The beach was another story. It was a few hundred yards long in a slight curve jutting out from the river. Our boats would land there and LST's

(Landing Ship, Tank) where the bow opens, and equipment can be driven off. Our boats were used to unload ammunition, food, PX goods, and C-rations. Forklifts could drive on and pick up the pallets usually stacked two high. An LCM could hold up to 60 tons depending on the type of cargo.

On the other side of the beach was a place situated for LCM's to be lifted out of the water by a gigantic 100-ton floating crane for dry dock. This allowed for any holes to be fixed, painting and screws (props) to be repaired. Also, each LCM used old rubber tires for "fenders" on the port and starboard side. About 6 or 7 tires were hung by cables on each side with a couple on the stern. Getting dry docked was not something I wanted, as it was hard work plus under constant scrutiny until ready to go back in service.

Now the beach was a place you didn't spend much time in. You brought your boat in, the Beach Master, usually a 1st or 2nd lieutenant, would come on board, check your loading papers, take count of the pallets, and then order it unloaded. His job was to constantly roam the beach to ensure everything was done with high priority and properly. The coxswain or the engineer (we were on the job trained to also operate the boat) was to keep the boat running at all times with a slight forward throttle to keep it in place so it wouldn't broach (turn sideways). If by chance the operator dozes off at night, someone would yell or blow an airhorn to wake him up. This was always good for a great razzing. Also, the C.O. had a reputation for driving his jeep around on the beach and canned docks looking for violations.

Being tied up during the daylight hours meant you better spend that time doing normal maintenance, repairing rope, emptying the bilges, and working on the engines and filter systems. Because the engines had a lot of miles on them, it was imperative to maintain them constantly to keep them running. Each boat also had a villager on board during the daytime, to do menial tasks. He was a great help, especially chipping paint off the deck, repainting, and splicing rope together.

In the outer harbor, which was actually part of the South China Sea, was where most of the cargo ships would be anchored. Sometimes a dozen or so would be anchored out there. This was a difficult job for the LCM operator to accomplish when it came time to unload the ship. Carefully using the two throttles, you would maneuver it alongside and hold it in place with throttles while a stevedore would be lowered down to help unload. His job was to help the crane operator place a pallet properly and then loosen the cable each time. This was not an easy job as a load had to strategically be placed to maximize the load and also keep it balanced. Ammunition was vital as sometimes there were different kinds, howitzer shells, bullets, mortars, etc. Of course there was the usual beer, soda pop, and c-rations which was easier.

One of the worst loads to get was bags of cement, which usually occurred about once a month. Invariably some of the bags would be punctured and spill into the well and then get wet. If it wasn't cleaned up immediately it would harden. That was the job of "Papa San" to do. Also, because this wasn't a high priority item, it could sit on your boat for a day or two.

I mentioned the Papa San earlier, as being a great help, but that wasn't easy. First there was a language barrier, also they weren't really ambitious. I always got along good with my Papa San, probably because I treated him like a human being. Many soldiers abused or ridiculed theirs to the point of almost being criminal. Most was verbal but I witnessed an occasional shove or pushing the back. I just couldn't do that, as I was brought up to respect one another. Most of them were polite, to the point of being very shy and apologetic, very withdrawn and small in stature. They certainly didn't deserve abuse just because they were different from us. Now, we did call them "Gooks" and "Slopes" which I'm not proud of now, but it was a part of our language. I didn't call them that to their face.

When it came time to eat, I couldn't watch what they ate. They carried small metal pots which usually contained fish parts, rice and some kind of vegetables. Watching him squat and eat that along with the horrible smelling sauce didn't help my appetite. Then when he was finished, he would chew on a couple of betel nuts, which even the women chewed. These were nasty and would turn their teeth black. One time I was offered one, but when I shook my head no, my Papa San just laughed.

Speaking of lunch, ours was bad enough. It consisted of opening a box of C-rations and heating one of the cans on one of the engines. I found out quickly that the best meal was Beans and franks or spaghetti and meatballs.

Once heated up it was at least edible. I thought of those poor souls in the jungle who had to eat their cold. The worst meal was ham and eggs chopped, which I had one morning. It looked like a spoiled omelet when opened and didn't smell much better. After heating it up, I gave it a try. Perhaps the rough seas didn't help because within an hour I threw it up overboard. I refused to ever try that again.

A case of C-rations contained 12 individual meals in a cardboard box. There was boned chicken, pork, ham, and beef along with some kind of potato or side dish. Also there was a spongy biscuit, a small can of peanut butter, a small can of jelly, a round piece of nasty chocolate, a small package of generic cigarettes, and the best can of all, fruit (peaches, pears, or fruit cocktail). There was also packaged coffee in the case. Our mess kit came in handy as it held our metal utensils and opened into a small tray with a lid. Usually we threw the small cans into the water and watched how far we could make it skip.

One of the soldier's best items was also in each case of C-rations, the famous "John Wayne Special" or P-38. This was a small flip open can opener with a hole in it to place on your dog tag chain. This device not only opened cans with ease but also doubled as a small screwdriver. What a great little invention which I should have kept. I do have a facsimile, but it's just not the same. Looking back at it now, I don't remember our Papa San ever eating any of our rations. I guess he was smarter than we thought.

One time our boat took on a load of K-rations, no doubt left over from either WWII or the Korean War. Some were stamped with the year 1943 on the top. It may seem hard to believe but our modern military had no trouble trying to feed soldiers food that was over 25 years old. Pretty disgusting. Of course we did open one up and tried it, and it was not much different than our C-rations. However, the canned fruit was moldy.

Some fat cats in the states probably got a promotion for saving the government money by using about 200 tons of this crap. I can almost hear his saying, "Hey, they can eat this stuff over in 'Nam". I hope whoever authorized that shipment chokes on his food every day.

Climbing out of the engine room

Two Vietnamese women begging for some C-rations

Bryson McGill standing at the bow of an LCM

My first boat, the 23, called Mr. Lonely after the song

CHAPTER NINE

LONELINESS SETS IN

It takes a while to settle in, get into a routine, get used to my surroundings, the adjustments that had to be made, but shortly thereafter, loneliness sets in. It really hits hard when during mail call happens and guys around you get letters and you don't. This was infrequent for me, but I had my long stretches.

My first letter from home took about a month to arrive, this is because I wrote as quick as I could to give out my new address and by the time they got it, and sent a reply almost a month went by. If a soldier didn't do this quick enough mail could of course take longer. Mail from home is what gave the soldier in Vietnam the extra will to live. The letter didn't have to say much, just a few words could be good enough. Little details of what mom, dad, wife, girlfriend was doing was read over and over again until a new one arrived.

At times I ended up with so many letters to answer it would take days to do it, and they would be fairly short. I had that special box in my footlocker for all my letters. I kept a rubber band around them to separate them from others.

Many times mail calls would happen just before we were ready to get on the truck for the night shift. When this happened, the truck was abnormally quiet as those who got mail would attempt to read them on the bumpy ride. Those wooden fold down benches and the dust from the road rolling into the back of the truck didn't make it easy.

The worst part about getting letters was finding the time to reply back. One thing the military stressed was keeping your family informed. The C.O. said he didn't want to get a notice from the Red Cross because your family had not heard from you. Writing positive letters, when possible, was also stressful to let your family or wife know everything was alright.

Numerous times after a 12-hour day I wanted to just kick back and relax and didn't feel like writing letters. The night shift was usually the best time to write, as you were less busy and didn't have to worry about a last-minute ship to go to. However, the lone light bulb in the wheelhouse wasn't that bright, plus you wanted to get an hour or two of nap time. If my buddy was sleeping, I would stay awake by writing and watching. We always found time to go to the PX, drink a beer or two, and play some cards to relax. Going into town for gifts, grab a bite to eat or just to look around was also needed sometimes.

My parents sent me a small AC/DC reel to reel tape recorder around December of 1966 which helped greatly. I asked for this type because it used batteries rather than plugging it in, because the current wasn't great because it was generator driven, this was obvious as the light bulbs in the hootch would brighten and go dim at times. Keeping D cell batteries in supply wasn't always easy, but I managed, because if I didn't the recording was bad. I also asked my sister, Barb, to create a rock and roll tape for me to listen to too. I would often play this in the hootch when playing cards.

Making tapes wasn't always easy, I quickly found out. It had to be a quiet place in the hootch which was almost impossible. If there weren't guys talking, it was the outside noise, planes landing, helicopters flying overhead, etc. Sometimes I would be interrupted by a house girl using her little straw broom as she swept up the dirt on the floor. I would sit on the edge of the bed and in a low, quiet drone-like voice make a recording. Sometimes this would take a day or two to fill the small reel up so I could mail it off. The real reward was getting one back so I could actually hear the voices of my parents and family members. That would sure make the tears flow.

Nighttime was the loneliest part of the day, especially on the boat. Between naps, writing letters, and just watching, there was complete pitch darkness and silence. Having too much time to think and reflect wasn't too sweet as your mind would drift away. I had that brightest star in the sky to look at like my mother told me to do and just talk to her. I tried to explain to her that there was an exact 12 hour time difference, noon at home meant midnight in Vietnam. No bright star for her to look at too. Sometimes I would walk out on the little walkway to the ramp and sit out there so I could verbally talk to her. That was peaceful and necessary for me.

All letters were not good letters. There was the occasional "Dear John" letter a GI would get. It was estimated that the 1098th got at least one of these letters per week. Hard to believe but it was probably true. Needless to say, there is nothing as crushing as receiving one of those letters. Most were from girlfriends, which is to be expected, but some were from wives.

I can speak firsthand about getting and also sending a "Dear John" letter. The one I received was just after Christmas from Lynda Bixler. I had sent her a nice jade ring she requested a few months earlier, so I thought everything was good. I was naturally crushed and walked around in a stupor for about a week and was very subdued. I confided in McGill and he helped me through it. I can understand now, as she was a senior in high school, quite attractive, and I was over in Vietnam. All those school activities and all those boys asking her out was just too much temptation, I guess.

Getting that letter from Lynda was probably my just reward for writing one to the girlfriend I had back in Saginaw. Again, I won't mention her last name, because it doesn't seem right, but Yvonee adored me and was crushed. Her long letter back to me was heart wrenching. I sent an eight-page letter explaining that it wasn't fair to her to wait for me as I had changed and was no longer in love. I never mentioned Lynda Bixler, as that would be nasty. I saw no reason to bring that up, but it was something I should have done face-to-face when I was home on leave, but I didn't have the guts to do it. Yvonne wrote me another letter after that, but I wrote a short one saying we both had to move on, and I was sorry. I never heard from her again while there, but she did end up marrying a guy I knew from bowling years later and she was happy and became a schoolteacher.

Many of the soldiers who received a "Dear John" letter from their wife, were absolutely crushed and probably contemplated suicide. One did upon arriving back home we found out later. His wife wrote saying she no longer loved him, found another guy, and didn't care if he ever made it home. He went to his local church and hung himself, we were told.

Of course, the best letters were the humorous, crazy, and sometimes very sexy ones. The funny ones you shared with others, and they would too. If someone got a sexy one, they would just say it and give a wry smile. Jimmy

Johnson was different however, he loved sharing his sexy letters from his wife, Eunice, and needless to say, we enjoyed hearing them. She would describe how she was going to make love to him when he got home, but Jimmy stopped with any details. Sometimes she would talk about taking a bath and being naked and thinking of him and had her girlfriend take pictures of her in sexy poses. He never showed us the photos. We would beg him for a glimpse or a few words, but Jimmy would just laugh and put the letters or photos away. She loved driving him crazy and he loved it as well.

Just about every waking moment between guys was about talking about home and something that happened or a memory. The card games were more quiet but once in a while the conversation drifted back home. A coxswain and an engineer got to know one's personal life pretty well, even though we were placed on different boats with a different soldier a few times.

My footlocker covers with my favorite girls and girlfriend

CHAPTER TEN

FIZZIES & GOODY BOXES

One of the greatest little inventions I took for granted in Saginaw, actually bailed me out in Vietnam. Fizzies! These were little pills of different flavors which dropped into a cup of water would come alive effervescently changing the putrid, disgusting tasting water into something palatable. I would never drink the water from Vietnam, but we had a huge water tank on wheels were I could fill a canteen or plastic glasses. I remembered those Fizzies and asked for a bunch of them to be sent to me. As a kid I would sometimes place one in my mouth and have it kind of "explode" inside. It was pretty neat.

I asked mom to send me Fizzies as quickly as she could after I got that first dose of that water tank. The little miracle pill would change it into orange, cherry, root beer, or grape drink almost instantaneously. I went through those by the dozen. The only present from home better than Fizziers, were "Goody Boxes". These were gifts from heaven itself, as they were packages from home or relatives packed with homemade cookies, breads, sausages, little cakes, etc. They were a soldier's dream meal. My sister sent me many homemade peanut butter cookies.

Whenever a soldier got a "Goody Box" he would come into the hootch, yelling, laughing, and requesting everyone to gather around and help share the contents. This was the ultimate food, but don't touch what a soldier liked best. Getting one of these boxes meant there was no need to eat in the mess hall. We would share in the goodies until they were all gone or needed to be saved for another day. Most "Goodie Boxes" arrived around holidays, with Christmas being the biggest pay day. I think I counted that I received 32 of them during Christmas time.

Ice cream was another major treat that was unheard of, probably because it wouldn't last long. I was able to barter for 5 gallons of the premium delight once from a ship. Wheeling and dealing for precious cargo were a common occurrence for our boat company, usually between the navy and Koreans, who drove the many trucks. Yes, it was called the black market, but we call it necessity. Ice cream was a necessity.

Remember an LCM carries about 60 tons of cargo, and each pallet is marked on a log sheet by the stevedore and the coxswain when loading is finished. I would say 90% of the time, these numbers matched, but there were times when they didn't. A smart coxswain or engineer would also count the pallets as they were being loaded along with the contents. Making sure there wasn't an under shipment was imperative, because that meant problems when unloaded. Now an over shipment was fantastic.

PX goods, beer and cigarettes were premium shipments. These items moved quickly because everyone wanted them. These were the items you looked for as over shipment. For instance, one pallet of beer contained 60 cases, and each case could be sold to Mama San or a local bar for $24. Of course, the markup on that case was at least double or triple that. Just contact a Korean truck driver, convince him a 50-50 split and viola, the pallet was gone and sold. Now when you quickly figure this out, it's a nice tidy profit; $24 times 60 cases equal $1,440 and divided by two equals $720 for the Korean truck driver and $720 for the boat crew. Now I'm not admitting to being involved in any of this, but bartering and sharing was necessary, and these goods were needed. As we said amongst ourselves, "Hey, it wasn't my fault they over shipped".

Let's get back to the ice cream story. My boat, the 23 at the time, took on a load of cigarettes and there was an over shipment. One pallet of cigarettes is a lot of cigarettes. These were usually not sold but shared with the other boats to use for bartering either with ships or with the company. Now for the navy, cigarettes were still hard to come by. So we pulled up next to one in the inner harbor and yelled at someone on board. They knew what was up and a couple of sailors came down the stairway on the outside of the ship and asked, "What have you got?"

I answered, "cigarettes".

The sailor said, "Great, what do you want?"

"Ice cream and lots of it"

"OK, will trade 5 gallons of vanilla ice cream for 20 cartons."

The deal was quickly made and now we had 5 gallons of melting, delicious ice cream to share. I can't remember which one of us came up with the idea, but it sure was a great one. Five gallons is too much for two guys, so we quickly got on the radio and told them to pull alongside, tie up and bring some spoons. You never said what you had because the radio could be heard by everyone. You just wanted your buddies to know, there might have been a code word or two also. Four or six soldiers can make quick use of melting 5 gallons of ice cream. Scooping it right out of the carton or into your mess kit and dripping it all over the deck was crazy. It was the only time I had ice cream during my entire tour.

Don't forget we also had lots of cigarettes to share also, so that was given out also. One other time we got an over shipment of PX goods. The pallet contained binoculars, cameras, radios, and the like. Once again, the stuff we wanted was kept and then the "code words" went out and we tied up at night with other boats and the bounty was shared.

There was another time when the entire company benefited from over shipment. Another boat was involved, and I don't know how it all came about but I know the C.O. was involved. The entire company had a huge steak BBQ one night and the captain said he didn't want to know where, how or what was involved, just enjoy.

It was easy to figure out that some kind of premium over shipment was involved and some navy ships benefited by just trading about 100 steaks. That was also the only time I had steak in the country. The benefits of over shipments on cargo were immeasurable.

CHAPTER ELEVEN

RESCUE MISSION

Life in the 1098th wasn't always working on boats, playing cards and drinking beer. There were times when missions were done, guard duty was needed, yellow and red alerts would occur, and then there was the rare rescue mission.

This rescue mission occurred about two months after I arrived. The entire company which was not working on their shift was told to fall out in front of the captain's hootch. Now we were all curious as this had never happened before, but we had an idea it was serious. About 35-40 men were huddled around the small, raised porch to hear what was up.

The First Shirt came out and he was dressed in full combat attire. We looked at each other and wondered what crisis had happened. We listened intently as he informed us that one of the two huge 100-ton cranes had broken loose from its mooring and had floated away during a freak storm and crashed into the rocks inside the harbor. He said it wasn't totally confirmed but the crew apparently was under small arms from the hills surrounding it. The crew was holed up and a waiting rescuing.

Now the captain spoke up and he was looking for volunteers for a rescue mission. A soldier's number one concern in Vietnam is his buddy, but the next priority is his buddy or another soldier. It didn't matter if it was his best friend, close acquaintance or a total stranger. It made no difference. They were "brothers" and needed help.

In a matter of seconds, the 1st Shirt had more than enough volunteers. I didn't even get the chance, as I paused for a second or two and that was it. There were six volunteers, all ranked soldiers, some in their second tour, chosen out of the dozen or so who stepped forward. They were told to get their weapons, dress for combat, and be back for the ride to the dock ASAP. They would receive details on the ride there. We were then dismissed.

Pulling off a rescue of this magnitude would not be easy. It involved taking one or two of the LCM's in very rough seas and bringing it alongside the crane which sits on a huge barge. This would be tough enough in the open water, but even trickier still when you think it is on the rocks and waves are probably crashing over it. If the crew was under fire, then it definitely will take some planning.

Here is what we found out when the mission ended. The rumor about small arms fire was false, but all the other details were true. The huge 100-ton crane did indeed, crash into the rocks and the crew was in danger of being washed overboard. The surf was banging the crane around pretty good, and it was in danger of toppling if it wasn't pulled away from the dangerous rocks.

The rescue was a frightening experience. After hours of trying to tie up to it so it could be possibly pulled away, it was fruitless. The men on board were already rescued as they had to jump on board the LCM, which was no easy task with a slippery deck and the boat bobbing up and down.

The next morning a couple of LCM's were dispatched to try and dislodge the crane from the rocks. The seas had settled considerably, but there was the unknown as to how much damage it had suffered. Although there were no gaping holes, there was a good amount of water in the bilges which needed to be pumped out. Once this was done the barge was at about a 20-degree angle, which added to the problem.

Tying up to the crane would still prove to be troublesome because of the angle. They wanted an LCM on each side, so once it was pulled free, it had to be turned so the other boat could tie up. Each boat used about six lines to tie up and they are about 3 inches thick. A couple of them came off or ripped, so it was good they had extra on board. It took most of the day to accomplish this feat and tow it to the area behind the beach used for dry docking of the LCM's. If you are wondering why a tugboat wasn't used, which would have been great, it's because there were none in Qui Nhon.

This crane was out of service for quite some time as some holes needed to be patched up. Having only one crane now meant we had to make sure our boats were operational at all costs.

CHAPTER TWELVE

THE CITY OF QUI NHON

Qui Nhon or Quy Nhon, was considered a safe secure large support base for the troops. There were times when that wasn't the case but not during my tour of duty. It is located on the central coast and is the capital city of Binh Dinh province. The population at the time was approximately 100,000 which strangely enough was comparable to Saginaw, Michigan.

One dangerous time was on February 10, 1965, when the communists struck as enlisted men's quarters with smuggled in bombs. The hotel like structure was leveled like a deck of cards collapsing. When the dust settled there were 234 dead and countless injured. This incident provoked president Lyndon Johnson to increase the bombing raids which were called, "Operation Flaming Dark".

Just seven months after I left the Tet offensive occurred on January 30, 1968. This was the Tet Holiday and a truce had been agreed to so the military was not prepared for the numerous assaults. Pleiku and Qui Nhon were hit hard and there were numerous casualties until the NVA and Viet Cong were defeated. The next night Tuy Hoa was attacked (just south of Qui Nhon) and the famous battle of Hue also began.

The sprawling coastal cities like Qui Nhon, Da Nang, and Cam Ranh Bay were extremely safe during the mid-60's which was perfect for the rear-echelon companies. These companies were housed in hotel-like settings or cement buildings. Not so the 1098th. Just about 35 miles north was An Khe, home of the 1st Cavalry, with Phu Cat just north of that with Happy Valley between the two.

Bong Son was located on the coast in the same province about 50 miles north. It was the site of a major battle in January of 1966 called Operation Masher. It was guarded by the 3rd NVA division known as Yellow Star. The

1st, 7th, 9th and 12th cavalry units comprising of almost 6,000 men, launched a "hammer & anvil" operation which would sweep the enemy towards blockading friendly units. On January 25th, a C-123 transport plane carrying 43 cavalry men crashed into a mountain during heavy fog. When Operation Masher ended, an estimated 1,358 enemy were killed, and 119 Americans died which included those killed in the plane crash. All in all, a very successful mission.

During the war the 1st Cav would battle the NVA again and again to keep control of the Binh Dinh province out of the hands of the communists. Some of the heaviest fighting would take place in An Khe and Pleiku and just over the mountains surrounding Qui Nhon. Of course some of the worst fighting was near the DMZ where Khe Sanh and hamburger hill was located. Highway 1 ran the entire length of Vietnam down the coast. Highway 19 went from Qui Nhon through An Khe to Pleiku. There were constant battles to keep these main supply routes open.

Many times, at night just beyond the hills, it was like the 4th of July. I would see the flashes of light from our compound or the boats as the sky would flash all around from the constant bombardment going on. Sometimes green and red tracers would light up the sky also along with the thunder like shells exploding. Helicopters would fly back and forth all times of the day and night, from the 85th and 67th medevac units with the wounded. I realized Qui Nhon was secure only because of those brave fighting men just a few miles away. God bless them.

The highest point in the city itself was the Catholic church which was situated at the end of a road leading into the city from highway 1. This was very visible as we rode each day. The downtown bustled with lots of traffic, mopeds, bicycles, and a few vehicles. There were bars and restaurants everywhere with Vietnamese and French names above on hand painted signs. Lots of outdoor stores were inviting as the owners begged you to see their wares of anything imaginable. Many satin jackets hung with dragons and maps of Vietnam on the back. So many handmade items by the people and each one was in competition with the others, so it was easy to wheel and deal. I bought two large dolls dressed in Vietnamese dress for my two nieces, Kimberly and Wendy, as they were still little. I sent a blue silk jacket with a pretty a pretty design on it to my dad. My brother requested a silk tie or shirt and for some reason I never got around to buying one. I regret that to this day. I bought various other gifts for my family, mostly as Christmas gifts. One I regret not buying was a small village scene carved out of ivory, with a small little bridge over water. It was beautiful, and now that ivory is no longer used, it would be rare.

Because there were a few isolated incidents of a soldier getting beaten, robbed, killed or perhaps kidnapped, my buddies and myself rarely ventured into town at night. The daytime was the best time for shopping. Many GIs went into town at night for drinks and whores, which were plentiful. Many times, a small boy would walk up and say, "my sister is number one boom boom, 10 dollars". This meant she was available for sex for just $10. Of course, with some bartering, it could be lower than this price. Where this occurred was usually in some back room on a musky mattress on the floor, with or without a sheet. Many GIs weren't worried about cleanliness, they just wanted sex.

I have to say many of the "bar girls" were quite pretty, some were Chinese. They would walk around wearing silk mini dresses in flashy colors. They would sit at your table as long as you continued to buy them "Saigon Tea", which was basically, water or plain tea. An occasional hug, kiss, or squeeze of your thigh would occur as they said all kinds of sweet things. Although most of these girls were prostitutes also, some were just hired to keep the soldiers there to spend their money.

Perhaps it was because of the married guys I hung around with, like McGill, that I didn't get involved in these activities. Oh, there were times I would enjoy a drink with a pretty girl, but it never went any further than that. We frequented a restaurant or two, which reminded me of the movie, "Casablanca". The tables had white tablecloths and a single candle burning in the middle. The main dish was usually a "steak" or a meat sandwich. I use the term steak loosely, as I'm sure it wasn't real steak. The meat sandwich was pretty chewy and tough, probably monkey meat we found out later. It was still better than C-rations. Unfortunately, dog meat is a delicacy in Vietnam, so I tried to be careful, and hoped I wasn't eating that. I certainly asked when ordering.

I had to save a dog from certain consumption once. Two boys were trying to pull a dog through some barbed wire near the canned docks. One was wielding a knife and was probably going to slit its throat. I hustled over as I was walking by and yelled at them in Vietnamese to let it go. When this didn't work, I knew I had to throw a big enough scare into them. I took my M-14 rifle and in a threatening way, yelled "Di Di Mau", which meant "Get Away". They were hesitant to let it go but figured it was best. I sincerely doubt I would have done anything, but they didn't know that.

A ride into town was always necessitated by jeep usually, but we returned by a bicycle pulling a little two seat cart behind driven by a Vietnamese. These were everywhere and fairly cheap. There was a small village around our compound with little dilapidated shops and homes, but I stayed away from them. We were informed the VC may have frequented that village at night. Many of these shacks were made out of cardboard or flattened cans, with dirt floors and a rug or two thrown over it.

The walk from the canned docks to the landing craft beach was a short 10 minutes with many small shops on the one side of the road. On the way the kids would flock to a soldier begging for any type of goodies. I carried some C-ration chocolate or cans of peanut butter with me for those times and would toss it to them. As the old saying goes, "kids will be kids".

Mama San would get our business at times like this. There was always the need for a can of pop or ice to keep things cold. Pop was a dollar, a can and a block of ice surrounded by sawdust in a burlap bag to keep it from melting was also a dollar. Of course, you had to keep taking the burlap bag back or the cost was more. Once on the boat a pail or metal locker was used to keep the pop cold. Ice was a major commodity, and it wasn't always available. It was fairly opaque and quite dirty, but it did the job it was intended for.

While the LCM was sitting on the beach waiting to be unloaded many times a small boat rowed by boys would come near and they would beg for goodies. We made sure they kept their distance for the fear they could be booby trapped. Just tossing cans of peanut butter, a biscuit or chocolate would usually do the trick. We were not allowed to give them C-ration food because that could be given to the enemy. Some guys would viciously throw these cans at the kids, which would make me sick. There was no need for that, but the anger and hate for being in Vietnam consumed them I suppose. When they hurt one, they would laugh. I didn't find any humor in it, but reasoning with them didn't work and I had to just ignore it.

Another reason why we were not allowed to hand out the large cans of C-rations was because the VC would use them for improvised explosives. This type of can was sturdier than an empty pop can and a grenade with the pin pulled, could be placed inside and tied to a branch or tree with a trip wire used to set it off. Just picture a soldier going through the jungle and having this happen. The VC wanted to disable a soldier rather than kill them, because it would usually mean one or two others had to take care of him. That put three out of commission rather than just one. The peanut butter cans were only about an inch high and basically useless for a weapon. The chocolate candy was sealed in a plastic foil of some kind.

It was always hard for me to believe children could be involved in any vicious act, but we did hear about it happening. They looked so poor and innocent, but I could never live with myself if I found out my can of food may have cost some soldier and arm, a leg, or worse yet, his life.

CHAPTER THIRTEEN

THE FIRST PURPLE HEART

Guard duty was another thankless but necessary job in Vietnam. Everyone had to pull their share of this. The only good thing about it was for an entire 24-hour shift which also meant you got 24 hours off duty when it was over. I had to serve on guard duty two separate times.

The guard truck would pick up the guards and drop you off at the guard barracks. A soldier would pull two hours on duty and then four hours off, where you could rest or sleep, rotating like this until the 24 hours were up. Sleeping on a cot wasn't that comfortable and it didn't help when guys would come and go or rather than sleep, would sit and chat or play cards. Trying to get a good, sound, hours of sleep was almost impossible.

There were various areas designated by our company to guard. One was the ammunition dump, which was a large section on the other side of the airfield, basically visible from our company. There were fuel oil tanks located nearby. They were round and about 30 feet high surrounded by dirt berms. The berms were there to contain any accidental spillage that could occur. Guarding the airfield was another duty which involved either walking along a barbed wire fence or sitting in the elevated guard tower at the end of the runway near the street. None of these duties were good, especially at night, when any sound or sight made you take notice or think awful things. You were completely isolated and had to remain alert at all times.

The oil field was pitch, dark with trees on three sides. The soft hot breeze would move the branches which would play tricks with your eyes and mind. I swore I saw shadows moving and I would stop and stare to make sure it wasn't somebody. I kept walking and being very alert while at the same time reassuring myself everything was safe.

Naturally guarding the ammunition dump was the least desirable job.

Although it was fairly secure being on the air force base and all, and situated between the airfield and the plane hangers, it was still the most likely target by the VC. It contained howitzer shells, boxes of grenades, M-14 and M-16 ammunition and bombs. Of all the places the guard officer would suddenly visit on his jeep, this was the most likely.

Sitting in the guard tower was probably the easiest of the three jobs I had, it was probably the least safe of all. I felt like a sitting duck. The tower was about 20 feet above the ground and a narrow built-in ladder was needed to climb up. Again, this was right next to the road inside the barbed wire at the end of the runway. The most traffic was during the day, but during the evening there was enough to make you aware of what could happen. Pedestrian traffic was never allowed to stop. I would shout down with the words "Di Di Mau" when someone did stop. Keeping awake was tough late at night and I certainly didn't want to be caught sleeping. That would be an automatic court martial.

It was during one of our guard duties that a GI from our company was wounded and received the first purple heart for the 1098th. The funny part was it happened while he was sleeping. An enemy bullet had pierced the tent covering and had lodged in his neck. He told us later he thought he just got stung by something. When he grabbed his neck the bullet actually fell out into his hand. He was embarrassed by all the attention he was getting.

The captain made us all fall out for the purple heart presentation. He gave a nice little speech and then pinned the medal on the guy. We all shook his hand afterwards and gave him some good-natured kidding. Who knows, maybe when he got home it turned into a good war story.

One particular incident remains with me that involved some strange guard duty. One evening a fighter jet attempted to land on our short runway. It apparently had run out of fuel and needed an emergency landing, rather than ditching the plane. The pilot did a masterful job with a full payload, but the metal planking blew his tires and he had to put it into the sand near the end of the runway. His big mistake was not dumping his payload into the South China Sea before landing.

There it sat, nose buried in the sand just short of the barbed wire with the tail sticking up and over the runway. Highway 1 was about 100 yards away and the Vietnamese were crowded about trying to get as close as possible to get a good look at probably their first jet fighter.

Within minutes our company was put on Red Alert, the highest alert possible, and we were told to fall out with our weapons and guard the plane. This was after our weapons were all confiscated and locked up in the arms room. The 1098th had many Yellow Alerts but a Red one was rare. Usually a Yellow meant an attack was imminent, and a Red meant one was either underway or close by. Having gone through these many Yellow alerts, I became complacent.

I took my time getting dressed and my boots on. I was one of the last guys to walk into the arms room for my weapon and ammunition. Then I found out all of the ammo was distributed, and I only had my useless M-14. I stared in amazement at the soldier and dashed out. All the time I was running to get into position, I was saying to myself, "This is crazy! I don't have any ammo!"

Being one of the last ones to fall into position in the sand, I was the closest to the compound but still a good 100 yards away. Soldiers were all in a prone position in the sand facing the perimeter. As they took positions, they spread out on both sides of the jet plane. It wasn't long before the captain came crouching up behind me as he was giving out instructions.

"How are you doing?" he asked when he got to me.

I replied, "I'm OK, but I don't have any ammo."

"What? Why not?"

"They were out when I got there" I guess I was expecting some kind of sympathy or something else.

"I sure hope you are good at hand-to-hand combat" was his reply as he left.

Those were not the words I wanted to hear. The guy next to me just smiled and gave me thumbs up.

Needless to say I was not in a jovial mood. I was not prepared for any combat let alone hand-to-hand combat. I'm still not sure if the captain was joking with me or was getting even with me for being one of the last in position.

It's a pretty eerie feeling laying there in the sand, it's in the middle of the night and the moon is shining brightly on us, and my weapon is worthless. I didn't even have a bayonet to fix. If an attack should happen, I laid there thinking of the possibilities I had to defend myself.

We spent the rest of the night guarding that plane and it was one of the longest nights I ever spent. One good thing about having no ammo, the captain didn't have to worry about me falling asleep. I was wide awake all night. I talked to the guy beside me, and we joked about it a little as daylight arrived.

CHAPTER FOURTEEN

30 FOOT WALL OF WATER

Working on the side of a ship is no easy task. The LCM has to be kept as close to the ship as possible for loading, and this could take a couple of hours to complete. Either the Coxswain or engineer would use the dual throttles to maneuver the boat into position. This takes quite a skill that both crewmen need to know, so one can take over, when necessary, especially for relief. McGill and I were getting so good at it, sometimes we barely rubbed the side of a ship. We were together on a boat for quite some time, which was pretty nice.

Bringing the bow in first towards the ship and then using one throttle and placing a prop in reverse and then the other throttle puts the other prop forward. By doing this back and forth, the stern swings into place and the LCM are now in position beside the ship. This has to be repeated continually to hold the boat in place until loading is complete.

A 60-foot boat would bob like a cork at times next to a ship, and depending on the cargo, there could be two LCM's working on the same side. This would take even more skill to hold it in place so as to not make contact with the boat either in front or behind. A stevedore or two would place the first pallet as close to the back of the well as possible and continue doing this until possible to start stacking on top. The boat could also be maneuvered back and forth to help with the loading as the stevedore's hand movements told the crane operator where to place the load.

Loading the second layer was especially tricky as the stevedore would have to balance on a pallet or two and coordinate with the crane operator. Quite a few times one would become injured due to a fall or getting hit with the hook. If the seas were rough, this was inevitable.

One time in particular we were ordered to work a ship in the South China Sea while a storm was brewing during monsoon season. Apparently, the person ordering this didn't realize what was close to happening. As we left the inner harbor the swells intensified from 10 feet high to 20 feet or more. The bow of the boat would rise up and then slam back down as the swell went underneath the boat. This was so brutal the whole boat would shake, and it seemed to want to come apart. As we neared the ship the swells got larger until they were either 30 feet or so. It got extremely scary at this point.

We tried to get the LCM next to the ship but then it really got out of hand. One gigantic swell would take us so high we were level with the deck of the ship and the next moment we would drop low enough to see the props of the ship. After quite some time of just trying to get a stevedore on board without killing him, we finally succeeded. You could tell the stevedore wanted no part of this. Whoever decided to do this either should have been onboard or shot.

Seasickness was starting to set in, which was strange, as we definitely had our sea legs. It must have been crucial for us to get this load of ammunition, because we worked for about 2 hours just to get about 6 pallets on board. Some of these got busted up in the process. Before long we called it off as more damage would occur and if the load shifted, we might sink. Getting the stevedore off took some doing, but he was able to put his foot in the hook and escape. I think the captain of the ship was ready to call it off also for the safety of his crew.

We radioed that we were coming back in with a partial load under very heavy and rough seas. Now our troubles were just beginning. As frightening as it was going out into the South China Sea, it was now far worse. Either the current changed or the wind, because now those swells were coming from the side of our boat rather than under the bow, and they were now about 30 feet or more. At times the stern would get hit hard and lift the boat up and then slam down with water washing anything loose overboard. However, seeing a wall of water as high as a three-story building, coming at our side time after time was like being on the Titanic. We felt like we were on a surfboard riding the pipeline. One moment the boat was on top of the wave and the next looking like we were going to be completely destroyed by a humongous tidal wave. Luckily, they would just lift the boat up from the side and go underneath. This was totally an awesome sight and I regret I didn't have a camera to capture it.

Getting back into the safety of the inner harbor and onto the beach would be a welcome sight. Most of our tires on the port side of the boat had been ripped loose or completely thrown over the side and into the well. Those on the starboard side, where we were next to the ship, were completely gone. Just the cables hung there like strands of hair. Although the engine room hatch cover was shut and clasped, the engine room had about six inches of water in the bilges. The room below the stern where the propeller shafts were located also had water in it. The pumps were working as fast as possible.

It took a while to unload the boat because the cargo had now spilled all over the well. Afterwards it took days to get everything repaired and in proper working order. Just hanging tires on the sides would be a real chore. The propeller shafts had to be re-packed as they were leaking badly, which took about four hours to accomplish.

About a week later we were dispatched to a troop ship along with other LCMs to pick up marines and drop them off on the beach to the south of the where we land to unload. They had no idea where they were going or if it was dangerous, for they were in the well and couldn't see over the side or bow. Most of them looked younger than we were and of course had that scared look, as they probably thought this could be like Normandy all over again. What would their first day in Vietnam be like? Of course, we knew they were going to be dropped off on a safe beach.

As we neared the beach, now hotels and buildings could be seen above the bow. They were no longer hotels, but at one time they were, maybe during the French occupation. This part of Qui Nhon was quite lovely, in fact there were civilians and perhaps some military sunbathing on the beach and having fun in the water. Quite a surprise to these marines when the ramp was dropped.

The second load of troops was not going to be as lucky. We were taking them around the point to be dropped off. This was more isolated and thicker with jungle and forest. I had an idea that platoon was going to get into battle soon. Because of the surf and possible low-lying rocks, we dropped the ramp about 25 feet from shore and they had to disembark by wading through high-high water. The big difference was they didn't have the VC shooting at them.

Our boat had a 50-caliber machine gun on board set on a tripod welded to the deck. I'm sure if we needed to use it, we couldn't have because the up and down motion of the boat would have prevented it. We made a couple more trips to the troop ship for troops before this was complete. I would say at least a half dozen LCMs were involved in this unloading process. I often wondered how many of these young men were never coming back alive.

Another incident involving my boat was when we got a load of napalm bombs on board. These were stacked sideways and were about 12 foot long, each inside of a wooden pallet, basically just 2X4's nailed together, so they could be unloaded by forklifts. Because these were napalm bombs, we had high priority for unloading.

As the forklift driver was unloading the last bomb, his fork punctured the side of the bomb, and it started oozing out onto the well deck. Now napalm is an incendiary mixture of a gelling agent and a volatile chemical. It is very gooey and sticky as it began to fill the back part of the well. The forklift driver came back with some ropes and a couple of soldiers to tie it off so he could drag it off. When I found out how he was going to remove it, I told him under no uncertain terms was he going to drag that bomb off my boat.

Before long the Beach master, a 1st lieutenant, showed up and came up to the front of the well deck and ordered the forklift driver to drag the bomb off my boat, as the crate was now damaged beyond repair. I told him, "You are not dragging that bomb off this boat. The only way is if it is carried off."

The lieutenant got irate and said, "Who do you think you are talking to? I give the orders on this beach, and this bomb is coming off now."

I replied, "As long as you are on my boat, sir, you'll do as I say, and I say it will not be dragged off. Now get off my boat."

"Let me talk to your commanding officer", he said angrily.

Now it should be noted that a ship or boat is in the command of the operator in charge of the vessel. In this case it was me. Although I was certainly out ranked by the Beach master, he has to get permission to come on board, and when on board, we are in charge.

I got on the CB radio and called my commanding officer. I said, "Sir, I have a napalm bomb on board which has been punctured by a forklift and it is split open, and the stuff is oozing all over the well deck. The Beach master now wants to drag it off my boat and I told him No!"

"He wants to do what?" the 1098th captain shouted.

The 1st lieutenant took the microphone and tried to explain the situation, and stated how insubordinate I was towards him and how I disobeyed a direct order. My captain stated over the speaker, "When you are on one of our boats, you will obey our orders. Now tell him to get off your boat and if he wants to come back, to ask for permission to come aboard."

I looked at him rather smugly and said, "You heard the man. Now, sir, get off my boat." I have to admit in all of my tours of duty I never felt better. I wasn't expecting that answer from my commanding officer, although I knew I was correct.

If wasn't long afterwards he showed up with another forklift truck and about 6 men. He almost walked upon the boat but stopped just short of the ramp when he saw me standing in front of the wheelhouse. He raised his right arm and briskly saluted while asking, "Permission to come aboard."

I saluted back and said, "Permission granted, sir."

The men the lifted the still dripping napalm bomb and gently placed it on the two forks. The driver then tilted the forks enough and lifted them so the guys could secure it with ropes. It was then carefully taken off my boat. They then returned with some sand and shovels. They dumped sand all over the good and were able to get about 95% of it off. What a mess.

I felt like I had won a battle, I have to admit. I smiled from ear to ear the rest of the day, and I'm sure that Beach master will never forget me. It took about a day of hard work by the two of us and our Papa San to remove the rest of it.

CHAPTER FIFTEEN

CHRISTMAS & BOB HOPE

Spending a holiday in Vietnam was the pits. Thanksgiving and Christmas are the two worst holidays to spend away from home, and in a war zone besides. Because we were not working (just a few soldiers were assigned the awful duty of staying with the boats tied up at the canned docks), thoughts of being home and how your family was celebrating the holidays without you was constantly on my mind.

A cease fire was agreed to by the United States and North Vietnam for these two holidays. A skeleton crew was needed to guard the boats however, and unfortunately, I was selected for Christmas Day evening. A crew of four was needed to guard about six boats tied up on the canned docks and another six tied up together in the inner harbor was guarded by another four guys. I ended up as one of the guards on the canned docks.

I did have Thanksgiving off, and we heard that the meal was going to be just like home, but few of us believed that. The joke going around was "How are they going to get a 20-pound turkey into a C-ration can?" We were proved wrong. The meal was served in the mess hall, and it was packed, and it was fantastic. A regular menu was given to everyone, turkey with all of the trimmings, dressing, cranberry sauce, mashed potatoes and real gravy, and even pumpkin pie. The cooks did a great job. Even the mess hall was decorated for Thanksgiving and real tablecloths were on each table. I ended up eating too much, but I wasn't alone. I even ate cranberry sauce which I never liked at home. I never saw so many happy soldiers in a long, long time.

Christmas Day was nice also, but we didn't have a meal like on Thanksgiving. A very nice meal was prepared but not that many guys showed up, probably because of so many "Goody Boxes" that arrived. In our hootch we all gathered around a couple of beds and footlockers and shared the wealth. My goodness, we had salami, bread, rolls, cookies, cakes and all kinds of pure junk food. One guy had a little Christmas tree sent and we set it up and placed a few decorations that were in the box on it.

Presents were opened up and showed around. There were some gag gifts which drew some laughs. Then we went back to write letters, take naps, or just enjoy some solitude to reflect on home. My tape deck played songs as loud as I could make it play. We made the best of our holiday.

That evening on guard duty I spent about an hour on the bow of a boat "talking" to mom. It was a near full moon so the area around us was pretty bright, but I still found the brightest star in the sky. I sure wish I could have called home, but I just used my imagination as to what it was like. My parents usually celebrated on Christmas eve by opening presents so we could go to church on Christmas day. I shed some tears and had a very quiet lonely night.

The next day was really going to be special for the 1098th and other military companies in Qui Nhon. The Bob Hope show was going to be at the airfield, and everyone was on a high note. Knowing Bob Hope always had some beautiful American female movie stars and dancers was what we really wanted to see. Bob Hope didn't let us down.

A large stage was set up on the other side of the airfield with a camera crew set up about 30 yards away to record it. This show, and others around Vietnam were going to be shown in America at a later time. Of course everyone wrote home to tell you where you were sitting or standing just in case it was seen. I was sitting about 20 rows back on the right facing the stage. I had my Polaroid, but I wish I had a 35 mm camera with a zoom lens.

Bob Hope opened the show with his usual routine, he came out with a golf club and had us all in stitches in no time. Then he introduced Miss World, a very lovely young woman from India, dressed in her native dress. There was the Korean Kittens, a dance group from South Korea who were fantastic. But when the real dancer, Joey Heatherton, came out we all went crazy. She is one gorgeous woman who can really shake it! First, she wore a short white dress but the 2nd time when she came out, she wore a black sequined mini-dress that had us all hooting and hollering.

Of course Bob Hope always had a little skit now and then to lighten things up. Billy Graham was part of the show, and he gave a nice little "sermon" and spoke about the meaning of Christmas and Christ and prayed with us. Anita Bryant, an excellent singer from America sang Silent Night to wrap up the show with all of those on-stage joining in. We all joined in as well, but it was tough as there were lots of tears shed.

As soon as the show ended, many soldiers shoved their way towards the stage to get a closer look, meet Bob Hope or hopefully Joey Heatherton. I was able to get close enough to shake her hand look at a true American girl again. I wanted to get a photo, but I used all my film up during the show, which wasn't too smart.

Later in my tour, Nancy Sinatra visited our company, and sang her hit song, "These Boots Are Made For Walking". Unfortunately I was on duty during the day shift and missed it. Of course I was filled in on everything, including how she looked in her white go-go boots and micro-mini dress. No details were left out about how sexy she was.

Joey Heatherton dancing on stage

Bob Hope show in Qui Nhon

Lucky for me, and many of my buddies, we had New Year's Eve off, and most hootches had some kind of party with lots of booze. The hootch next to ours where Jerry Arnett was living, was the chosen one. For those poor saps who had to work, because it was a full workday, we said "Cin Loi" which is Vietnamese for "Sorry about that".

Also in the hootch was a Hawaiian GI, who knew how to concoct the wildest, greatest drink ever. Just watching him pour fruit juices, fruit, and all kinds of alcohol, mostly rum, into a large pot borrowed from the mess hall. He then topped it off with a couple of pineapples. It was strong but absolutely delicious. It sure did a number on us though, I have to say I didn't have a hangover the next morning, which was good as I had to work.

Celebrating the New Year (1067) made everyone feel a little better, as it felt like a whole year was behind us. Some there were "short" (had little time left in country), some had just arrived a few weeks earlier, but most of us had about until June before we would go home. Besides the punch there were bottles of whiskey and many cans of beer.

Bright lights were strung about the hootch which blinked on and off at times as the power would surge from the generators. I had never seen Jerry

Arnett drink any alcohol before, so seeing him drink right out of a bottle of whiskey, was unreal. He was single and from the little town of Grab, Kentucky and was a true "good ole boy". Hank Hoeffs, Jimmy Johnson, John Handley and a Korean soldier joined in and were singing some kind of song.

After all of the drinking and partying it was late and mother nature was calling. I went out back to relieve myself in the sand near some sandbags. I thought to myself, why is it so bright outside? It was now morning, I was lying in the sand with a sandbag for a pillow, and the hot sun was beating on my face. My neck hurt from that sandbag and the side of my face was covered in sand. Wow, that was some night!

CHAPTER SIXTEEN

"DUCK, YOU ARE BEING SHOT AT"

New Year's Day is usually set aside to recuperate from the excessive partying the night before. Back home, football games would be watched on television. Not in Vietnam. Like I said in the previous chapter, I had to work and so did Bryson McGill.

It was time for our night shift, and although we were suffering a little, we did manage to get a lot of sleep. It was Sunday, and we went from an 18-hour day shift to our 18-hour night shift. Thank goodness for that. We were sent to get a load of cargo out in the South China Sea just after getting on board. We had a good 3-4 hours of daylight so it shouldn't be any problem.

After loading and heading back in, we always got a little closer to shore so we could round the point and enter the inner harbor. I was out on the deck and had just got done checking the bilge pumps to make sure they were working properly. Now on each side of the wheelhouse are small lights, the port side (left) uses a green light, and the starboard side (right) uses a red light. Just enough light to illuminate someone out walking on the deck. As I passed by the wheelhouse to climb inside, using the small opening I heard a "ping" sound. I thought I had dropped my screwdriver which I usually carry in my rear pocket. I grabbed the flashlight so I could look for it, which was not a good idea. Just picture me bent over next to a bright green light, with a flashlight, looking for something. Why not paint a large target on my back while I'm at it. It's a good thing we were a couple of hundred yards from shore and the VC wasn't a sharpshooter.

Almost immediately after turning on the flashlight, there was another "ping" and then another one. McGill, who was watching me while operating the boat, immediately recognized the sound and yelled, "Duck, you are being shot at! Mom didn't raise a complete dummy. I dove into the wheelhouse and landed on a small wooden bench behind Mac (my nickname for McGill). He had ducked down below the wheelhouse as well for protection and turned off the outside lights.

We huddled there for what seemed like minutes, trying to determine if what we heard was true and what we should do. Should we return fire? This was not a good idea as we didn't know exactly where it originated from. Mac turned the wheel, and we headed back out into the South China Sea full throttle. He grabbed the radio microphone and called it in, telling the C.O. that we had taken some small arms fire and the approximate location. We were told to get as far out of range as possible and take a different route into the inner harbor. I'm not sure if a reconnaissance patrol was sent or perhaps a helicopter gun ship. We watched intently as we entered the harbor and eventually landed the boat on the beach. This wasn't the only close encounter I had but it was the only one regarding enemy fire.

The other incident I was involved in was also a little scary. It occurred on a different boat with a different coxswain, We had taken on a load of bad flour from a ship, infested with bugs and spoiled. Now you are probably wondering how a load of flour could become dangerous, well, let me explain. One, the local Vietnamese were not supposed to get any of this flour for consumption because of possible disease. Two, the military didn't want to take a chance this could be turned over to the enemy, as it could feed them for weeks.

We took out a couple of other guys and about six Vietnamese to help unload it into the South China Sea. Now getting rid of about 20 tons of flour into the South China Sea would be no easy task. About half of the load ended up being loose flour and it was all over the bottom of the well deck. Bags would have to be ripped open and dumped overboard. Any loose flour would have to be shoveled overboard as well.

What happened next was totally unexpected. We had no sooner anchored, when we noticed little two or three person Vietnamese boats coming from every direction. How they knew what we were about to do, I don't know, but it was suspected they overheard the conversation on a short-wave radio, which many had. However they found out, doesn't matter, it just seemed like half of Qui Nhon was out there, wanting this load.

As they got nearer to us, and became a threat, the others and I grabbed our weapons and threatened to stay away. This was good for a few seconds, but as soon as the work resumed to dump it, they came even closer. Some tried to climb onto the downed ramp, which was level on the water, others were alongside the boat grabbing the tires hung on the side.

The desire for food was more important than their lives as it was now getting out of hand, or perhaps they thought we weren't really serious about possibly shooting them. Little did they know they were correct, as we had called in saying what was occurring and we were given specific orders to keep them off the boat by any means possible, short of shooting them. We also had to worry about the idea of some of them could be VC and could lob a grenade onto the boat.

The Vietnamese on board were communicating in a very boisterous manner to those trying to get on board, so we didn't know what was being said either. Starving, poor, hungry people will do desperate things for food, and this was now the case. There wasn't enough of us and so many of them as they now were on both sides and the stern, and some were on board already. We were shoving them overboard and shouting at them to stop. This didn't work, it only encouraged them more. They were like ants all over an ant hill. One eventually got into the well and grabbed a bag of flour and was attempting to climb out. He was briskly picked up and thrown overboard. Amazingly he never let go of that "white gold" he clung to, which became worthless when it got wet. Boats were converging on him to either rescue him or get the bag of flour, probably the latter.

It was obvious that more stringent measures were needed, or we would be overwhelmed. While the Coxswain was raising the ramp, myself and the other two soldiers decided to shoot holes in the bottoms of the boats beside the boat. We made threatening moves with our weapons first, in hopes that would work. When another Vietnamese got on board we had no choice. He was shoved off and then I emptied my clip into two boats, and one began to sink, the other two soldiers did the same. Of course we were cautious to not shoot anyone.

This seemed to work as now the flotilla moved slowly away and just drifted along about 25 yards away. Then they began circling like they were going to try again. We decided to just drop the ramp and rip the bags open and throw that into the water and worry about the loose flour later. As the six

Vietnamese on board did this, the three of us stood guard, with our rifles. This was working, and after a couple of hours the bags were dumped and useless. We decided to go full throttle further out into the South China sea and then shovel off the loose gooey flour. What a mess we had but it was gone. It was easier to get to the beach and using hoses, wash what was left out of the well deck.

I was never so happy to get a job done before. We laughed about it later wondering what kind of price we could have got on the "black market".

CHAPTER SEVENTEEN

HAWAII, HERE WE COME

If the unbearable heat isn't bad enough in Vietnam, then obviously the worst weather is Monsoon season. This is known as the wet season, which is a complete understatement. This season begins about late November and could last into the month of March. The really hard rain would occur early on and then be off and on for a month or two.

A better name would be "stay soaked and wet forever"! Just picture yourself in a shower fully dressed in the water turned on as hard as possible. That is a good description of Monsoon season. When it begins to pour in Vietnam, you are lucky to see six feet in front of you. You can wear a poncho, like most soldiers do in the field, but we decided to just endure our fatigue with no shirt on or a t-shirt on. During the worst time, the rain is relentless. It could go on for days and days, with the only break being steady rain rather than pouring.

I tried to stay dry when not working, but it was nearly impossible as everything seemed damp. The hootch even had that damp, musty feeling, and the bed felt the same. Trying to get a good sleep was trying, and then getting up and attempting to pull on your clothes was truly something else. Many times you wear the same wet clothes because why bother with dry ones when as soon as you step outside you are soaked. It was a rare day indeed when the sun would shine. When it wasn't raining, it was a cloudy, dingy day.

It also got quite cool at night. The average daily temperatures were about high 70's, low 80's and the night temperatures in the 60's. Now, that might not seem that cool, but after all of the heat, your body isn't acclimated, and a blanket was needed at night. It is not that unlikely for the coastal cities to average about 120 inches of rain during the season. That's about 10 feet of water! There were times when it felt that much was coming down all at once.

Mac and I decided months before during Monsoon season that we would take our R&R (Rest and Recuperation) leave in Hawaii. A soldier in Vietnam has a choice, you could stay in country and take it on some beach near Saigon, called the "Second French Riviera", or go to another country like Thailand or Australia. Another great choice was Hawaii! Since his wife was due to give birth to their first child sometime in March, Hawaii was the perfect choice, as he could call home at a smaller cost than the other choices. Some guys chose Hawaii also, because their wives or girlfriends could fly there and meet up with them. You were ordered not to go to the states from Hawaii.

My mother's birthday was March 12, so it was an easy decision to pick a week in that time span, a great opportunity for both of us. On January 31st, we put in for March 10-16, but too many already chose those dates, so we had to opt for March 3rd to the 10th. I have to admit another reason was to see some good-looking American girls in bikinis.

We miscalculated escaping from monsoon rain, as that ended about mid-February and now it was starting to get hot again. Thinking we could have been enjoying Hawaii during Monsoon season made us wonder about our mentality we would laugh about later. We weren't absolutely sure we would be able to go together, because plans could change a month later, but we lucked out.

When you get close to R&R you are basically worthless as a soldier. Your mind just isn't with it, but by keeping busy, time goes by much quicker. With just two days to go, we had our bags packed and we were ready and hoping nothing goofy would happen to prevent it.

On Friday, May 3rd, we got on a C-130 and headed for Cam Ranh Bay, About 125 miles to the south. This is one of the safest places in all of Vietnam as it seems to be surrounded by miles of sand. After a night's stay in the "plush" concrete barracks with running water and actual hot showers, we left for Hawaii on a Pan Am jet. Just seeing those pretty American stewardesses was pure joy.

The flight was a long one and it gave us a chance to take a nap as flying over the Pacific Ocean can be a real bore. Once again, a few cards games broke out to break up the monotony, but not for us. We landed in Honolulu and were disappointed that we didn't get the traditional lei greeting by hula girls. Those travel brochures sure lie.

From the airport we were immediately taken by bus to Fort DuRussell, and everyone was given an orientation. We were told to behave, do not get locked up and absolutely do not discuss with anyone any operation you are involved in back in Vietnam. We were finally told when to report to the airport for the flight back and to not miss that flight or you would be considered AWOL. We were then released to be on our own.

Well, after eight months in Vietnam, and not seeing any "round-eyed" girls, Hawaii is the place to be. There were beauties everywhere in bikinis, walking on the sidewalks, riding in cars, on Waikiki beach, and in the lobby of where we were staying. We got a room in the Reef Towers which overlooked the end of the beach. It wasn't the best room, but two soft beds, and a view was all we needed.

Once we got settled in our room, our immediate thoughts turned to home and Mac made the first call to his wife in South Carolina. While he was talking, I decided to go down to the lobby and check the place out. I had about 15 minutes to kill before I could call home. Just outside our room was a vending machine which sold pop and juice. I noticed a can labeled Papaya juice which looked pretty tasty, so I decided to try some, never having any before. What a delight! After gulping down the first can I bought another. To this day when I see a papaya in a grocery store or papaya juice, I reflect back to Hawaii. I really love the stuff.

It was now my turn to call home. It had been eight long months since I heard my parents, brother and sister and my hand was shaking a bit as I dialed the number. They were notified by letter prior, so everyone had an idea when I would call so they were ready. God, it was great hearing everyone's voice once again. Mom and dad were getting a little choked up talking and I truly wish I could recall the phone call, but I can't. After about 20 minutes, I said I would call again in a day or two and said what we were planning on doing in Hawaii. I do remember mom sobbing as she said goodbye and said she was praying for me to be safe. I made two more calls home before returning. I assured everyone that I was in a pretty safe zone and not to worry.

It was getting late in the day, so Mac and I decided to get a glimpse of Waikiki before it got dark. Like a typical tourist, I got a picture of three lovely girls in bikinis walking by us on the sidewalk. They just smiled and didn't seem to mind, perhaps our haircuts gave us away as soldiers. That photo was a real hit back in Qui Nhon when I showed some guys. Because it was getting dark, the beach was nearly empty, and we walked around a little more before returning to our room.

The next day we decided to rent a car and travel around the island of Oahu. What could be better than a bright red Chevy Chevelle convertible! It was a little pricey, but if you're going to ride around in Hawaii you have to do it in style. We drove past Diamondhead and just took the main route around the island. The beaches on the other side of the island were absolutely spectacular. There were few sunbathers but plenty of surfers.

Having no idea where we were driving to, we saw a marine land park and stopped to take that in. We watched a dolphin show, saw some sights, and then headed back to Honolulu. A few stops along the way were needed as another breathtaking view would pop up. Being with a happily married man and me ogling bikini clad girls was not a great match, but I tried to contain myself as we passed many again on the road.

One crazy incident took place that I have to mention. On the night before we were to leave, we took in what was a high class "burlesque type show". The girls weren't truly strippers, but true dancers with little on. I think I talked Mac into doing this. We were standing in a line waiting to go in as there was an admission charge and most of the couples were pretty dressed up. Now I had already had a few beers during the day, so I was a little lit up.

A man in a suit standing behind us asked if we were GI's. I tried to ignore him, but he insisted very nicely. I don't recall everything I said but Mac told me the next day, I was kind of nasty. Then the guy introduced himself and said he was the Vice President of the Dole pineapple company. I made some snide remarks about being someone important because I didn't believe him. He insisted on wanting to do something for the "boys" over there and wanted our address so he could help out. I ended up giving him my name and address just so I could get rid of him. I don't know why I was like that, perhaps the beer.

A few weeks after we got back the captain called me in to talk to me. Now, this was very strange, so I wasn't sure what to expect. He asked me if I met anyone special in Hawaii. I pondered a bit, and said no. He replied, you didn't meet the vice president of the Dole Pineapple company. I was a little startled and said yes, but I doubt that he was who he said he was. The captain stated that I must have made quite an impression on him as he was sending a truck load of fresh pineapples for the entire company.

Mac was pretty depressed, as his wife didn't give birth while we were in Hawaii, so now he had to wait for the slow mail to let him know. I can remember Mac paced the floor like an expectant father many time. When it finally occurred, on March 20, I do know it was a girl. He was ecstatic! We ended up smoking a cigar to celebrate. Mac was one proud Papa San!

CHAPTER EIGHTEEN

CLOSE TO DEATH

Death and dying is not a subject many veterans talk about, but it is something nearly everyone who has been in a war has experienced. Naturally most soldiers do not think they will be killed, it will happen to someone else, not them. I figure everyone in the 1098th was planning on returning home safely. Nothing really happened that said otherwise. Witnessing death was not common and I'm sue few did. I wasn't one of the fortunate ones.

I never thought I would see a dead body in Vietnam. Those type of horrors only happened in the bush. I have seen many types of sick and diseased people, many laying by the side of the road, but those were Vietnamese, and although it was sad, it didn't affect me as much because it was just "them". That may seem coldhearted, but it was a fact of life over there. Earlier in the week, we had learned that during a very dark night a navy patrol boat had pulled up next to a Vietnamese fishing boat to check it out. The two sailors on board either got a little careless, or perhaps were taken by surprise. They turned out to be the enemy, and an explosive of some kind was tossed into the navy boat and perhaps killed the two sailors as they were MIA (missing in action).

We were told to keep a lookout for any bodies floating nearby. Both of us spent most of the night shining our flashlights into the water searching for possible bodies and keeping an eye out for anything suspicious. It was a long and fruitless night finding nothing.

The real "fact of life" hit me pretty hard on a hot, humid night as we were tied up to the canned docks, waiting for a load of dunnage to be removed. That usually meant a night of leisure, so I was busy writing letters, and my coxswain was taking a nap. We both spent some time searching for the waters again, but decided it was time to quit.

A small navy patrol boat pulled up alongside our boat and a sailor yelled out for us to call an ambulance. As that was being done, he stepped on board and said they recovered the two bodies of the sailors and needed help getting them on board. The sight before me was truly gut wrenching. The two sailors had not only been gruesomely killed, but their faces were also badly mutilated probably from the fish eating their flesh. This is what can happen after being in the water for almost 48 hours.

It was a horrible, grotesque sight as I helped lift the bodies on board. Their bodies were pretty stiff and also shredded with shrapnel. Their flesh was a ghost like pale white. It took everything in me to carry them and not throw up. That would occur later. It was the only time I saw actual "death" over there. I thought about what those poor souls in the bush had to endure and witness during battle.

Although that was the only time I witnessed death, it wasn't the only time death almost happened. I almost died myself, I was told. The incident I'm referring to happened on a Friday, September 2, 1966, just over two months after arriving in-country. It was a freak accident, but it almost cost me my life.

The engine room of an LCM has a small opening just in front of the wheelhouse which is covered by a hatch cover weighing about 30 pounds with a handle under it to help pull yourself up. The top of this hatch cover has an eyelet where a hook is used to secure it to the wheelhouse. To get down into the engine room, I had to squeeze through this opening and climb down about three rungs on a metal ladder.

Before the engineer goes down into the engine room, either he or the coxswain secures the cover to keep it open. Our boat, the Foxtrot 23, (our company used the code word "Foxtrot") just picked up a load and was coming into the inner harbor and I went down into the engine room to check the bilges.

As I was coming out of the engine room I reached up, grabbed the handle to help pull myself up and pulled the heavy cover right down on my head. Either the cover wasn't latched properly, not latched at all, or it might have broken, I never found out what actually happened. I was knocked unconscious and fell to the engine room floor.

My buddy (I forgot his name) yelled at me to ask if I was alright. Hearing no response and seeing me lying there, he knew something serious had happened. He immediately got on the radio and called for an ambulance to meet us on the beach when we landed. Everything I will tell now was told to me later, by either the medic or my coxswain.

When we landed the ambulance was waiting and two medics and my coxswain helped lift my limp body out of the tight confines of the engine room and the small opening and out on the deck. I was quickly checked for vitals and placed on a stretcher and carried to the ambulance. This is nothing more than a glorified, olive-green 3/4-ton truck with a huge cross painted on it and equipped with all the necessary equipment.

I was then transported to the 85th medevac hospital. While on the way I had stopped breathing momentarily and I had to be given mouth-to-mouth resuscitation by one of the medics. This information was told to me by a nurse. She told me I was unconscious for about two or three hours and they were extremely worried about my life and condition upon arrival. It was then determined that I had suffered a very severe concussion and would have to remain there until I was ready to be released, which would be at least a couple of days.

While I was in the hospital, I witnessed many fellow soldiers who had probably been wounded in either An Khe or Pleiku and had been brought in by helicopter. It was sad to see some of the injuries. Mac came to visit me and said that I was in and out of it while he was there.

I suffered severe headaches while hospitalized and probably slept 16-18 hours a day. I didn't talk to any of the wounded around me, probably because I was in and out of consciousness. By Monday I was feeling much better, although I still suffered from severe headaches periodically. The captain talked to me about being either sent home or to the Philippine Island for recuperation. I didn't want to leave my buddies, so I told him I was OK for duty pretty soon. The doctor said he was going to release me back to my company for bed rest, because they needed the bed for the heavy casualties which were due in.

I was transported by jeep to the 1098th which didn't help my condition any, strapped into a bucket type seat and bouncing along. I think my head hurt more after that ride than it did before. The doctor informed the captain that I was to stay on bed rest for five days. I could then be released for duty depending on my condition.

Being on bed rest allowed me to catch up on my letter writing. I'm sure my parents were wondering why I hadn't written in over a week, so I wrote a quick letter telling them what happened, leaving out some details so they wouldn't worry. When I had to get up to use the latrine or to shower, I was a little wobbly and unstable. It took nearly a month before the headaches were almost all gone.

I am now finding out how much that concussion cost me health wise. I still have tingling fingers and some numbness in both hands. There could be other symptoms, but I really don't know.

The only other serious injury our company incurred that I heard of, was when one man on an LCM which was tied up together in the inner harbor, made a mistake and slipped and fell between the boats and was crushed. This happened when the waves would bring the boats together.

CHAPTER NINETEEN

VIETNAM'S 1ST AMPHIBIOUS TANK LANDING

It was now late March, and I was becoming a real "short timer"! I had less than 90 days to go so now I could "officially" yell "SHORT". What a great feeling that was. However, rumors were floating around that our company could be sent south for possible river patrol in the Mekong river. Those are some of the most dangerous duties for a boat company. I thought, "Man, I'm not ready for that."

We knew that our boats would be perfect for river patrol, the flat bottom could easily navigate the shallow waters and the boats could also carry cargo as well as land troops. The boats were already armed with 50 caliber machine guns on the starboard side, so it would be easy to place another on the port side. Also, the decks would be perfect to stack sandbags on for added protection.

We also knew the bad points about using an LCM. They are slow, and too large to make an easy turn if needed, which made them an easy target. Mortars or rockets could easily blow one out of the water.

The other rumor going around was we would be heading north, up the coast to land troops, ammunition, and possibly tanks. Needless to say, we were somewhat relieved to find out the latter rumor was true. How far north we were going and what kinds of landing would we be making? If tanks were involved, it could mean a difficult landing.

We were assembled at night on the movie theatre grounds and told of the upcoming missions. The captain informed us that we would be making numerous landings up the coast in the next few weeks. First to Bong Son and then to a little-known place called Duc Pho, located in the Quang Ngai Province about 75 miles north of Qui Nhon. He proudly said, "The 1098th was going to take part in the biggest amphibious landing since World War II.

Heavy artillery units were in both of these places. This province was where the 1ˢᵗ Corps was located. Chu Lai and My Lai were located just north of Duc Pho, as well as Dragon Valley, both huge battle zones, which made that a more likely place to drop off troops and tanks.

There would be several landings in the next few weeks, maybe months, with most of the landings at Duc Pho. Once we returned there was little time before the next mission would take place. The strongest and most seaworthy boats with the best engines would haul two tanks and the M-60 type tank weighs about 40 tons fully loaded with a crew of four. This was a surprising announcement because we were told an LCM had a 60-ton capacity. It was going to be a busy month or possibly two.

Not much information was relayed to us as to the exact whereabouts of the drop zone. We had no idea how secure the beach was, what kind of bottom was there and just how close we could get to shore. The next couple of days preparing was hectic to say the least. First sandbags were strategically placed about 3 high around the deck and the 50-caliber machine gun mount. Boxes of C-rations and ammunition for our M-14 were also taken aboard.

I no longer had a Mac for my partner, and neither one of us was about that. I did get lucky and got Gary Pollock from our hootch, so at least we knew each other. Gary was a very young looking 20 years old operator who had only been in the company for a few months. Both of us being from the Midwest we have a pretty good connection.

Because this was a two-day event, both crews were used. Fred Gray, who was also from our hootch, and a black guy named W. A. Stewart who I wasn't that familiar with were the other crew members. The only time I saw these guys was when I came on board for shift change. It made for crowded conditions on board, especially for the wheelhouse, so the two coxswains would remain in there and Stewart and I would remain on deck. This would be an ideal set up because it would allow for some nap time as each crew could relieve the other.

The first mission would involve eight LCMs carrying 10 tanks to Bong Son. For those boats the loading would have to be done very carefully and with great precision for balance. The well deck could barely contain these two tanks, and too much weight in the bow could be disastrous in the open sea. The 45 and 63 were chosen for this heavy load.

My boat was the 65 and we would carry one tank. The tank was backed in with even space on each side for balance. The tank we carried had a crew of four who we never saw, except for the driver. That was strange. They carried a red cooler strapped to their backs, which I also found strange, it was like a bull's eye in my opinion. Boxes of C-rations, extra tread, wheels, and other gear was also strapped on both sides and the rear.

Each boat was loaded in the pre-dawn hours and then sent into the outer harbor where we would all assemble when loaded. The trip was long and arduous thanks to the heavy weight and the seas. Because of the heavy loads of the 45 and 63, their speed was reduced meaning we had to throttle down to the same speed. We might have been going at 10 knots tops.

Since this was our first trip up the coast and the furthest, we had ever gone was maybe 5 miles up, the view became very different quickly. We needed to stay about two miles off the coast so we wouldn't catch any small arms or mortar fire. Unfortunately, this also meant for rougher seas, and a real burden on our diesel engines. The engine room had to be checked constantly and the bilges pumped continually. You could just feel the strain on the boat. I'm sure that was why we didn't see the crew of the tank; they were probably seasick.

Traveling those first few miles in near darkness was also strange. When the sun began to rise, it was a pretty neat sight. The silhouettes of the boats with tanks as the Sun rose and the sky turning blue was awesome.

It took about 10 hours to finally arrive off the coast somewhere near Bong Son. The 65 was the 5th boat and we had to look for a large red banner to help with the landing site, just point the bow at that. Because of the nature of what we were carrying we had to be aware of any enemy fire, land very quickly, dropping the ramp at the same time as we hit the beach. As this was happening the tank was already starting to move forward slightly so it could just roll off and get off the beach quickly as well, which was located about 100 yards from shore.

We spotted about a dozen men on the beach giving direction with hand signals to the LCMs and the tanks. Lucky for all of us, the surf was fairly nice which made for a pretty smooth landing. We now needed to back off quickly so another boat could arrive. The entire landing probably only took about an hour to accomplish. The only problem we had was avoiding the 57 which got a little too close to our port side.

PHOTO OF BOATS HAULING TANKS

The return trip was mostly done in pitch darkness which made for an eerie night. You could hear the boats and see their running lights, but not the actual boat. Radio contact was to remain silent unless there was an extreme emergency. Except for a little small talk among the four of us, and the steady drone of the engines, it was very quiet. It was time for some sleep, so that was accomplished in shifts.

We arrived back at the canned docks as the sun began to rise, bringing a new day. There were two trucks there to take us back and when we returned, we ate some chow and went to bed. The next mission was to begin in the pre-dawn hours once again, but we had to prepare also.

I often wondered how those tanks and the men on them made out. What was their mission? How many survived? I would never know, but I sure wish those very brave men the best.

destroyer pounding the beach before we landed with tanks

myself Behind 50 caliber Machine gun.

CHAPTER TWENTY

FOUR MORE MISSIONS

Duc Pho would now become a common word around the 1098th Century. We would continue to take trips up the coast delivering ammunition and supplies for the 1st Cav. Each mission would be quick and upon returning just a day or two before the next one began. There would be just enough time to sleep, refuel and load up again. It was going to be a very busy and trying month.

During these missions I think I wrote one letter home, but not to anyone else. We were just so busy, and I just wanted to spend some time relaxing and playing cards was another way to do that. Sometimes just writing a letter becomes a chore. It was great getting letters but not writing them.

Once we got to our boat, we proceeded immediately to the fuel barge for refueling. You always wanted to be one of the first in line because it took so long as only two boats could be refueled at one time, and that took quite a long time. A crew would rather sit on the beach to unload than out in the water vying for a spot to just refuel.

The first mission to Duc Pho consisted of just eight boats again. Every boat this time carried 60 tons of ammunition except for the 54 which carried a fork lift for unloading and a few other supplies. Our boat, the 65 was fully loaded with 155 howitzer shells. It gave me an uneasy feeling knowing we were going to an unknown site, probably pretty remote, with 60 tons of ammo onboard. It's like sitting on a huge bomb. One direct hit and there wouldn't be enough of you left to put in a jar.

Once again in the predawn hours, the two forklifts worked quickly and carefully as they laid down three rows of pallets, about five feet square and containing about 40 shells, and then nine to each of these three rows for 27 total. They would eventually stack another three rows of eight each for 24 on top of these for proper balance. Once loaded we proceeded to the outer harbor and waited for the rest of the boats. This would be an even longer mission as it was almost twice the distance, and we would be lucky to go as fast as 6 or 7 knots (1 knot is equal to 1.15 mph).

After about 10 hours we arrived near our destination, either a cruiser or a destroyer was spotted in the distance, a few miles offshore. It was ready to clear the surrounding area of the beach with heavy shelling. All the boats were now located between that ship and the beach awaiting word to land. Because we were located in that area, we were the ones getting the brunt of the sound of those guns going off, was ear shattering. Sound travels until it hits an object and that was us.

The shelling went on for about 10 or 15 minutes and we could see great plumes of dirt and sand on the beach and just beyond as the shells hit. This meant only one thing to us, the beach was not that secure, and my hands got a little sweaty. I shoved my clip into my M-14 and then checked the 50-caliber machine gun just in case it was needed. We all put our steel pots on our heads and started in for the beach. Two boats would land at the same time, get unloaded, then the next two would go in. The 54 would be one of the first because of the forklift.

Just as we started to move in, the next sight was truly awesome. Two fighter jets came in from the north, swooped in over the trees, and dropped their payload. Another pair of jets came in shortly afterwards, dropped bombs, shot their rockets, and then quickly disappeared. Their precision bombing into the tree line was so neat to watch. A small mound to the south of this area was untouched so we figured this must be where our troops were located. If anything or anyone survived the shelling from the ship and these two bombing runs, they would have to be one of those "super roaches" from our hootch I said, which made us laugh.

The 54 landed first followed by the 45 and then our boat. We knew this was going to be time-consuming with just one forklift, so we were glad to be one of the first. The surf was pushing against the stern, so Gary Pollock had to keep maneuvering the throttles to keep the boat straight. If the boat started to turn, it could mean trouble, as it could broach (turn sideways). If this happened it would be all over and stuck on the beach.

It took just over an hour to be unloaded, and small arms fire could be heard in the distance. Other than that we encountered no enemy fire. I'm certain the ship and the jets took care of the problem. Howitzers and men were seen in the distance with sandbags set around their guns. I was sure glad when that last pallet of shells was unloaded, and we got off the beach safely.

Darkness was now setting in, and we waited for the 54 to get the forklift off the beach to be taken back. We were told to get as much rest as possible on the return trip, because once we got back, the next morning we would be going back again. At 3:00 a.m. we were getting on the trucks to go to the canned docks and our boats. Once refueled, we went to the beach for loading. The 57 this time would be taking the forklift and supplies. We got another load of 155 howitzer shells stacked the same way.

This time we had an idea what to expect so we got a little more rest and ate some C-rations. It was humorous to see Fred Gray get a lifejacket for a pillow and stretch out on a pallet of shells and fall asleep. I got a spot in the shade behind the wheelhouse and used a few lifejackets for a bed and a pillow. After a few hours we took over the controls and let Pollock and Stewart sleep.

As we got closer to the beach it was obvious the beach was much safer this time. There were three howitzer placements on the beach, and they were heavily sandbagged. There was no need for a navy ship or jets this time. The 57 landed first followed by the 70 with assorted pallets of ammunition and then the 59 went in just to the right of it. We pulled in next to the 59 and when the 70 was unloaded and it pulled out. Things were going smoothly until the unthinkable happened.

I could see on the 59 that they were having trouble with the forklift. Men could be seen scurrying around and looking at the forklift, and I knew right away this was not good. After about a half hour they were able to get it running again and had about half of the load off the 59 when it happened again. After what seemed like eternity word got to us that the forklift was broke beyond repair, and the 59 would have to be unloaded by hand. About 10 men were recruited to accomplish this difficult task trying to finish before dusk settled in.

The sky was turning grey and then the quietness was shattered by a mortar exploding on the beach about 100 yards away, just to the right of our boat.

Pollock was able to catch the other blast just after it occurred with his 35 mm camera. That was enough for me, like myself, and I think Fred Gray jumped over onto the 59 and helped John Handley and the rest of his crew unload it. We were sitting ducks and I wanted off the beach.

Those were the only mortar explosions on the beach so someone must have taken care of it. Now it was our turn, and it was no easy task unloading 155 howitzer shells which are quite heavy. First each pallet had to be broken into so each one could be carried off via a "bucket brigade". Each was handed off through about a dozen guys to stacked as best they could. It was well past midnight when the 65 was finally unloaded and after almost 7 hours, the crew was exhausted. We finally pulled away and waited for the other boats to be unloaded in the same manner.

It was way past 3:00 a.m. when the final boat was unloaded, and we were able to start the long ride back. The good thing was that the boats were empty except for the last boat hauling the broken forklift back, which meant we could go full speed. Why only one forklift? One had to stay back for unloading. An LCM had a top speed of 10 knots, cutting our return time to 7 hours. It was past mid-morning when we tied up at the canned docks and almost noon before we ate and went to bed. Except for the naps we grabbed, we had basically been awake for about 32 hours, and we were exhausted and some of us had trouble falling asleep.

The day had ended but we had another mission to fulfill and that meant another 3;00 a.m. start again. Same routine and then we were on our way. No ammunition this time, instead we were loaded with JP-4, these were large, rubber-like fuel pods shaped like barrels. This time only six boats were involved as two had to go under repair for engine problems and bilge pump problems. The 57 was used once again to take a different forklift.

The 65 carried about 25 of these strange looking fuel pods. We were told they were to be needed for helicopters. They were double stacked on the well deck which made a visual problem for the coxswain. The entire trip took place with the operator unable to see the bow of the ship, so he got help from one of us, which wasn't that bad, as each boat kept a pretty good distance. The forklift had to make some strange maneuvers to unload these pods, but it went off without a hitch. This was the most uneventful trip we made.

Once rested, we found out the next trip was going to be our last. Nobody was heartbroken over that announcement. This time the 65 was to carry the forklift, C-rations and pallets of burlap bags used for sand bagging. The beach at Duc Pho had grown from three howitzer placements to seven. Ammunition was carried by the other six boats.

As we got near the beach, we saw an unfamiliar sight, this time a LST was unloading on the far end of the beach away from where we normally land. A BARC was traveling with us, which is an amphibious boat with large 8-foot-tall tires to allow it to go on land and it was to remain for some reason.

Because the surf was determined to be too rough to land, we were told to tie up to another boat and wait. We sat about a mile offshore and tied up to the 57, which had a fairly light load. We decided to go swimming, so the crew of the 57 dropped their ramp to level and we stripped down to our undershorts and had a ball. I, Paul Chiarelli, Billy Campfield, Pollock, Gray and Stewart enjoyed the cool azure waters of the South China Sea. We finally got a chance to swim in it. We wished we had some beer as we sat on the edge of the ramp.

About an hour and a half later we were told the surf was not going to get any better so we had to go in and do the best we could. Because we had the forklift, we were the first to attempt a landing. As we got about 30 yards from shore and it was getting treacherous, the boat was getting slammed and when it rose up, the boat wanted to turn sideways, and it would broach if this happened. Pollock immediately put the props in reverse and the strain was enormous. The boat shuddered but held up and we slowly backed away. Pollock circled about 200 yards out looking for a better opening.

The 60 and 68 were sent in and tried to use the LST as a barrier. This helped somewhat but the boats were still pushed away from the ship, but they were finally able to land. Each wave could be seen breaking over the stern of their boats and against the wheelhouse. They held steady and radioed for us to hurry and land so the forklift could unload them. The 65 tried the same maneuver and Pollock did a masterful job of getting the boat into position, by using the LST and we came in next to it. He slammed the throttle forward and we lurched and with the waves pushing into the stern, we slammed onto the beach. We were now worried that we might have gone too far onto the beach and may not be able to get off.

At times the stern would rise up and slam down and other times the surf would crash over the stern against the wheelhouse. Both hatches had to be closed tightly to keep the water out. Perhaps a sand bar had been built up from the previous landings, and this invisible barrier was more ideal for surf boarding than landing a boat. The ramp was dropped, and the forklift drove off and went to work immediately unloading the 60 and 68.

Now the 55 were attempting to land and with great difficulty. At times the bow of the boat was hovering over our wheelhouse as the coxswain attempted to use our boat as a buffer. All four of us were crowded in the wheelhouse now, and we were pushed forward each time a wave hit the stern. I swear Pollock lost 5 years of his life which made him only 15 now. Then the shout went out, "There they go!" We looked over just as the 60 and 68 broached. They were now sitting sideways on the beach and being pounded by the waves.

The 60 were outside and were getting the brunt of it all. The spray would shoot about 25 feet into the air. The crews of both boats scrambled on the slippery decks to jump off safely, which was difficult to say the least as a few of them fell down and had to crawl. They made it over to our boat, soaked, scared but safe.

Because our boat was carrying the least needed load of C-rations and sandbags, we were to be unloaded last. I decided to get off and take my polaroid camera to get some pictures. This was the first time I took my camera, and it was only because it was supposed to be our last trip and I wanted some pictures. What a great decision that was, as I got some photos of the 60 and 68 as well as the howitzers on the beach.

Finally, after what seemed an eternity, our boat was unloaded. As the load lightened, it became increasingly more difficult to hold the boat in place. Once again Pollock did an outstanding job to keep it from broaching. The empty boats must have been the cause of the 60 and 68 to broach. Pulling away from the beach was going to be a miracle. We decided to leave the ramp down to use as a stabilizer so we wouldn't broach, this turned out to be the best decision. We were also about 5 feet further onto the beach so backing off would take all the power we could muster. The engines and props were taxed to the fullest and we slowly began to pull away from shore. I don't have a clue how we did it, but we finally were able to get out far enough to turn and go out into the sea. With the other crews on board, we breathed a huge sigh of relief.

The 55 was not so lucky. After it was emptied, a huge wave slammed into the stern, lifting it, and the boat turned and broached. We now had three boats stuck on the beach. Of the seven boats who had made the trip, three were broached but unloaded, ours was safe, two others were on the beach getting unloaded and one was awaiting orders on what to do. It was obvious to all of us who got away, those two boats on shore had maybe a 50-50 shot at getting out. It was decided the one remaining boat would not try to land and within an hour, the two on the beach miraculously pulled away and joined us. The four boats now limped back to Qui Nhon and would be looked at closely for a possible damage.

Once back at our company, the captain had a decision to make. Could any of the broached boats be salvaged and pulled off the beach. The next day the 65 and another boat with Billy Campfield on board would travel to Duc Pho and meet up with a large tugboat and attempt to dislodge the boats from the beach. If they were deemed too heavily damaged, then any parts worth salvageable would be taken off. The 60 and 68 were so heavily damaged that their wells were full of water and not worth the effort. I took a photo of Campfield jumping into the water of the 60. The 55 was deemed salvageable, although the front of the wheelhouse was split in half and with some effort by the other boat and the tugboat it was pulled away and undertow.

Now for some more bad news. The 55 went into about a 30-degree list and began taking on water. Before long it had flipped and now was being towed underwater. Hard to believe but it was pulled to a salvage ship that way. Now the 55 needed s\e serious repair work.

The last trip truly was memorable, and I know the entire 1098th was glad it was over.

Billy Campfield jumps into the
water off the broached 60

Billy Campfield jumps into the
water off the broached 60

LCM 59 and 70 being unloaded

Me sitting on 60 tons of 155 Howitzer shells
Howitzer placement on Beach

CHAPTER TWENTY-ONE

SHORT!!

Recreational activities of the 1098th were usually just card games, watching movies at night, drinking contests, and an occasional game of catch. Near the end of March someone organized an intramural football league. It was a six-team league consisting of men from the 1st platoon, 2nd platoon, MMAV, maintenance, HQ, and the "lifers" (sergeants and officers).

The team ending up in first place at the end of the "season" would get $100 which would be used for a "Short-timers Party". It was a double elimination tournament, which meant a team had to lose twice, and our platoon, the 1st, won our first game 12-0. I would write home and say this was the most fun I had since arriving in Vietnam. It was short lived, as we lost our next two games and were eliminated.

The "field" was laid out next to the airfield and was 60 yards long. Since we played in the sand under the extreme sun, the games were played in late afternoon or early evening under a shortened time limit. It was two hand touch but a lot closer to tackling football, very physical and competitive at times.

A person wasn't considered a "short-timer" for this unless he had 60 days or less to go in-country. By the time our last mission to Duc Pho was over and April had started, I was getting "Short". In a letter home, dated April 21, 1967, I had 59 days to go. I now had the right to yell this at any time.

In that letter I wrote that the heat was really getting unbearable again, close to 105 degrees. "I'm getting a nice tan anyway", I said. In fact, I was so dark I could have passed for a full blooded-Indian. My skin was the color of mahogany. I also asked dad if he ordered my car yet. My cousin, Donald Schimpf in Flint, had a great job at Buick, and said he could get me a 1967 Buick Riviera at cost. It was to be completely loaded, gold in color with a dark green interior. I had been sending a $100 money order home every month (this was great on a $244 monthly hazardous duty pay) to help with the down payment. I had to sell my '65 Chevy Impala SS when I got drafted so some money came from that. I wrote, "I want dad to pick it up for me and have it setting in the driveway when I get home." I also wrote that the 1098th was still supposed to move to Saigon, but because I was short, I probably didn't have to go with them (I don't know where I got that idea).

The month of May closed in, summer was coming here, and I wanted out of here. Now, something would occur which would make my job even better. The company had a roving engineer, someone not assigned to any boat, just would go from boat to boat and help troubleshoot. He also would go to a disabled boat and take parts off it if they were needed. The captain called me into his hootch and offered me the job. I stood before him as he explained in detail everything that was expected of me if I accepted. He said I was highly recommended for the job by my platoon sergeant and said a few other flattering comments. I really felt good about this until the "hitch" came.

The captain said, "How would you like to make sergeant? This would mean more pay and prestige. Just think, you would make sergeant after only being in the army for a year and a half."

My mind was racing at these comments, and I thought Wow! "How do I get to be sergeant?" I asked.

"All I ask is for you to extend your stay in Vietnam for 90 days. You would be given a 90 day early out and discharged from the army when you leave Vietnam. What do you say," the captain said.

Spending even one extra day in Vietnam was not something I wanted to do. I only had about 45 days left, and I wanted to go home. I looked the captain right in the eyes and replied, "With all due respect sir, you could make me a full bird colonel and I wouldn't want to stay here one more day". He kind of smiled at that reply and said he respected my wishes. Then he surprised me with these words, "The roving engineer job is still yours if you want it." I said yes, he congratulated me, I saluted and left.

Those last days I would spend in Vietnam were now going to be so much better for me. No more missions, long shifts at night, and no more shipments on a boat. Those night shifts were actually not bad, but now I could just sleep in my own bed rather than in some uncomfortable place on a boat. Working days would now involve working with another engineer on a boat if needed or working with a rookie engineer who just arrived.

One day in particular a boat blew its exhaust system on the port side and was in need of another. This system consisted of two long pipes, heavily insulated, extending out of an engine. It was about 3 feet long and quite heavy and mounted in the middle of the engine room wall and it was vented out through the side of the boat, just below the deck.

I had to go to the 55, which had been towed to the canned docks about a week earlier. It was basically useless, as the wheelhouse had to be totally replaced and the hull was in need of heavy repair. The engines were flooded with salt water and basically no good, but there were some parts that were salvageable. The exhaust system was still good, so I decided to use this.

I showed the engineer on the other boat how to disassemble his exhaust system while I did the same. It was extremely hot in the engine room of the 55 and

I was sweating profusely. It was probably about 130 degrees down there and many times I had to come up for fresh air. Hanging on to tools was quite an ordeal also, and they became extremely slippery, and the sweat would run into my eyes, which didn't help at all.

What should have taken maybe two hours maximum to remove, ended up taking most of the morning and part of the afternoon to accomplish. I only had a flashlight to help me, as there was no power on the boat to light up the two bulbs in the engine room. Once removed, I helped the other engineer to install it on his boat. We were able to do it within an hour and just before shift change.

I had a few jobs similar to this but most of the time I worked as an advisor which was pretty good duty. I was also able to take a hot shower whenever I wanted and take a break to write letters. When June arrived, I had less than three weeks to go. I wrote the following letter home.

Our orders came in. I'll be leaving here on the 20th of this month and flying to Cam Ranh Bay via troop plane. Then the next day I will be leaving Vietnam by Pan Am jet to Seattle, Washington. When I get there, I have to turn in my fatigues for khakis and summer greens. I guess they look pretty sharp. I will probably spend the night there and then take a plane to Chicago and then Saginaw. After my leave, which should be 45 days (30 days plus 15 days travel), I will be stationed at Fort Story, Virginia. I don't know what I'll be doing there.

Just think, I wrote, only a couple of weeks to go. Just two lousy weeks and this long year will be over. I sure miss everyone a lot. More than ever. It won't be long. I guess I better get going. I won't be able to send a tape so I will write a short letter in a week. Until then, remember I love and miss all of you back home, more than you can imagine. Say hi to everyone. Love, David.

I was now on cloud nine. All I had to do now was to clear the post, which involved going to certain areas, like maintenance, headquarters, etc., and carrying papers for someone to sign.

I should have known it was going too smoothly. Disappointment arrived when I found out the port calls didn't come through. I wouldn't be leaving for a few more days. Some of the guys that came over with me were leaving every day. It became very depressing to say goodbye and still be here.

Finally my port calls came in and now I was the "shortest guy in the 1098th". My tour of duty was finally coming to an end.

Me Saying Short to Handley

CHAPTER TWENTY-TWO

HOMEWARD BOUND

One of our favorite songs we played almost every day was "Detroit City". Now, most of the guys were from all over the country, but that song had a famous line which we would all sing out together, "Homeward bound, I wish I was, homeward bound." I could now sing that phrase with some real meaning. The day had arrived, and I was leaving.

The night before, I had carefully packed all my clothing and other items in my duffle bag. I had already sent my Polaroid camera and tape recorder home along with my letters and the photos I took. I also took all the photos off the inside lid of my footlocker and sent them also. I had a huge smile on my face as I took the calendar hanging on that wooden crate and I placed a big X on the last day.

The hard part was saying goodbye to all the guys in the hootch who were staying. Caleb Collins and Gary Pollock still had about six months to go, and it was tough saying goodbye, especially to Gary as we had been through quite a bit in the last couple of months. Fred Gray was working, so he wasn't available, and the rest of the guys were gone already. We hugged and shook hands, I wished them the best, and none of us had dry eyes. I knew I would never see these guys again and the apple in my throat was getting large.

I left the footlocker next to my bed for the next guy to have, threw my duffle bag over my shoulder, took one more look around and headed out. As I walked along the wooden sidewalk, I looked briefly into each hootch and yelled "So long" as loud as I could. I said goodbye to the guy in the post office and told him if any goody boxes came for me, he could have them. I then climbed into the jeep which was taking me to the airfield.

I glance over my shoulder for one last look through the dust at the 1098th. The trip to the airfield was a short one, I shook the driver's hand, wished him well, and waited for instructions to climb aboard the C-130. There were a few other guys leaving as well, so there were smiles all around. We were heading for Cam Ranh Bay, and then America.

I stayed in a wooden barracks in Cam Ranh Bay, and we were separated from those who were arriving, so that was great. After eating a decent meal, I walked around the base a little as I was getting anxious. I notice a guy with a duffle bag walk up to a huge dumpster and throw his bag inside. I asked him why he did that, and he said, we were getting new clothes anyway, and he didn't want any remembrances of Vietnam. Then I did something I regretted later, I went to my barracks, grabbed my duffle bag and dumped it as well. I took out photos, and anything of personal value first. Oh how I wish I would have kept some of the clothes and the boots.

The night seemed to last forever. I spent some time talking to the guys who were also going home, but I didn't sleep much. Morning came and I boarded a Pan Am jet, which needed to land in the Philippine Islands for refueling. I sat back and enjoyed the rest of the flight to Seattle, Washington and of course took a nice long nap.

Landing in Seattle was a fantastic feeling because now I was back in the good old USA. I would receive some bad news, however, my connecting flight to Chicago, would not be available for another 12 hours, and my seat was not guaranteed. I decided to book a flight the next morning instead. I called Hank Hoeffs, who lived in Seattle and before he left about a week before me, told me to call him if I had a layover. Once I told him of my predicament, he and his wife came and picked me up, I got a little tour of the city and spent the night at their house and enjoyed a great home cooked meal.

Morning came, Hank gave me a ride to the airport, I said my goodbyes, told him I would write, and soon boarded a jet for the long trip to Chicago. After about a five-hour flight, I landed at O'Hare airport and transferred one last time for MBS airport to Saginaw. It was getting to be early evening now, and between flights I called home and gave them my arrival time. It was only a short flight home, perhaps about an hour or so.

I had to walk outside to board the small prop plane for the trip home, and I'm not sure my feet even touched the ground. The plane was almost empty, only about 20 people on board. I was the only soldier on board, as the stewardess welcomed me aboard with that beautiful smile. I got some smiles as I walked down the aisle in my dress khakis and medals on my chest. I found a seat all to myself, nobody next to me, and got comfortable next to the window.

Flying over lake Michigan as the sun was setting was pretty neat and when I finally saw the flickering light of residents on the shores of lake Michigan, I knew I was almost there. The stewardess asked me if I wanted anything to drink and I replied, "Just milk, I haven't had milk in over a year." She returned and asked if she could sit next to me for a while. How could I say no to an American woman? She was very sweet and asked me a few questions about Vietnam, but mostly what it felt like to be going home. She was having a layover in Saginaw as well. She sure helped me with my nervousness and seeing those beautiful round eyes was a blessing.

The moment arrived and we landed, taxied to the terminal which I didn't recognize. When I left, they were building a new terminal, so I left from the old one. I was one of the last persons off the plane, and as I walked to the many people awaiting me inside, I touched the ground and looked up and thanked God. Mom was the first person to greet me, and she just gave me a big hug and cried. It was very emotional, as I hugged my dad, sister, brother and a lot of relatives who showed up. Even my cousins from Hemlock were there. I thanked them all for being there for me.

I had to briefly sit down and take it all in. I was mentally and physically exhausted and looked at it, I was told later. I don't even remember the ride home. I still had 42 days of leave left and I was going to make good use of it.

The old two-story house on Maine Street never looked better. My room never looked better. I slept like a baby that night. I was home!!!!

My '67 Buick Riviera sitting in front of my home

CHAPTER TWENTY-THREE

MY LAST MONTHS IN THE ARMY

Being home on leave with my brand new '67 Buick Riviera was awesome. The car looked even better than I imagined. I had been in contact with Pat Keech, a girl who used to date a friend of mine. She had written to me and told me to make sure I looked her up. We had quite a few dates, and frequented the gravel pits in Vassar where most young people went to swim.

Of course there was a lot of time spent with family and friends. Strangely enough I hung out with seven guys in the neighborhood growing up, and never got a letter from any of them and while at home none of them stopped by. I don't even know if any of them got married or took jobs out of the city.

I was having so much fun I actually lost track of how many days I was on leave. This was not good, and then the rioting broke out all over Michigan. Detroit was burning down, the national guard was called in, and I believe dozens of people were killed. Saginaw had riots also, but not as destructive as Detroit, but they went on for a few days.

I said my goodbyes to everyone, including Pat, and drove my car to Fort Story, Virginia. When I arrived, I was immediately summoned by the company commander. He was pretty upset and wanted to know why I was late getting back. He said he was going to send an MP to pick me up because I was AWOL for five days. I had no idea, but I thought pretty quickly of a possible excuse. I mentioned the riots that were going on and he said he saw them on the news. I also stated that I couldn't get out of town because I felt it was unsafe, and it almost worked, except he then said, "Were your phones out of order too? You could have called!" I thought for sure I was going to get Article 16 and be busted.

He was actually pretty good about it, which was shocking. He said "You do know you have no leave time left; in fact you owe me. Don't ask for any because the answer will be no." This would prove false in October as my grandmother died, who lived with us, and my mother contacted the Red Cross who contacted the captain. He called me in and said if it wasn't for the Red Cross and the fact that my grandmother lived in our house, I would not be allowed to go home. He had some sympathy and gave me a Five-day pass as I would be driving. It was very kind of him after what happened back in early August.

Fort Story is a very small fort right at the end of Virginia Beach. It is located not far from the Norfolk Naval Base. There were two large light houses on the base and the barracks were two story wooden ones. I have to say it was pretty easy duty, which I will explain later. Quite a few of my friends ended up here as well, Jerry Arnett, Mac, Campfield, Johnson and Les Cimino from Baltimore. I ended up hanging out with him quite a bit as Mac would use his weekend pass to go home, and Campfield and Johnson lived in Virginia.

Les and I spent a lot of free time on Virginia beach girl watching and sometimes we would get lucky and get a date. Because of my fancy car, it was a "girl catcher". In fact I had the best car on the base, even the company commander, a colonel, drove a '59 Chevy Impala. Cars on the base were supposed to have a sticker on their windshield identifying if you were an officer or enlisted. Red numbers meant enlisted and Blue numbers signified an officer. It took almost a month before I was issued my red sticker and I cleverly put it in the shaded area of my windshield instead, hard to see. Whenever I would come and go, the guard on duty would salute me and I would in return, as he couldn't see my sticker really well and just assumed I had to be an officer. Before long, each day when work ended Les and I quickly showered and headed out.

We were put in charge of a group of guys who were not even privates yet, having just got out of basic training. We were specialist 4th class, and we gave orders and most of the guys were too scared to say otherwise, especially when they found out we came back from Vietnam. Most of them probably knew that was their next destination.

Most of the time the day would start working in an area where many "dummy" pallets were stored and used for practice with forklifts for moving and stacking. There were rows of these, stacked three high, about a 100 to a row. We now had figured out a clever plan, we gave the guys orders to move all of the pallets from one side to another area about 30 yards away. I said when we return at the end of the day, it better be done correctly. We then headed for the beach and would return by 4:00, and we repeated this often.

On the weekends, when it was still hot and sunny, the beaches were crowded, and Les and I would leave after work on Friday and be out looking for girls. We ended up convincing two beauties on the beach that we were college guys, not army guys because military guys were not really wanted then. So that night we went for a drive and had a few beers.

I made the mistake of not wanting to stop for a light and cut through a gas station to avoid it. Just that quick the red flashing light was seen in my rear-view mirror, and I pulled over. It wasn't the police but the navy shore patrol, who had authority also. He asked if I was in the military, and because we just lied to these girls, I had to say no, just vacationing. He asked to see my driver's license and low and behold my military ID was right in sight. I was caught but I was too stupid to just tell the truth, so I told another lie when he asked why I had that if I wasn't in the military? I said I was but was discharged and no longer in. Then he said, "If so, you should have turned that in." He took it and let me go. Now I knew I was in trouble but what could I do, but hope I get away with it. I didn't.

After spending the weekend with these girls, we returned to the base Sunday evening. Monday morning the captain, who was already upset with me for being AWOL for five days called me in. He asked where I was over the weekend and if anything strange happened. I tried to get out of this mess, but he quickly reached into his drawer, took out my ID and slammed it on the desk. He said, "Don't you ever, EVER, give up my military under any circumstances! Do you understand? You're lucky I can't stand those 'Squids' (what army guys called sailors)." He handed it back and that was it. I saluted and with my tail between my legs, hurried out of there.

Once the weather cooled down a few weeks after Labor Day, the beaches became almost empty. College students and high school kids were back in school, so we didn't go to the beach any longer. Les and I seldom made any trips into town, except for maybe a bar or two with some of the other guys. It was basically dead in Virginia.

Because Les lived in Baltimore, only about 150 miles away, he invited me to stay at his house one weekend. A weekend pass can only be used for distances less than 100 miles, and even Mac used his to go home to Woodruff, South Carolina.

Les had a very nice family and two sisters, Pauline, a senior in high school and Cookie a middle school student. Les had a girlfriend and we went to this bar to hear a band play along with Pauline. We had a great time, too good actually, as we stayed until midnight before driving back just in time to fall out at 6:00 a.m. This was repeated many weekends.

It was during one of these weekend trips that I met my future wife, Linda Marasa. She lived on Hartford Road; her father was a barber and her mother a hairdresser. and also had a brother, Pete. Les and I were invited to a house party and two girls caught my eye, Linda and her girlfriend, Gail Posey, were sitting on a couch in the basement and I squeezed between them. Before long I had made a date with Linda to go to the movies the next day.

Every weekend thereafter, I made that trip to Baltimore and would barely make it back by Monday morning. It was a ritual. Linda was a senior in a large high school and a few times I would show up in full uniform and pick her up. She said her friends were impressed with my uniform and my car. Linda and I got engaged when I got out of the army on Christmas eve, 1967, and married on July 7, 1968.

On my way to Baltimore I would take a black friend of mine to Washington D.C. and drop him off at his house. I never realized the bigotry in the south until I witnessed an event firsthand. I had stopped for gas in Richmond on the way to D.C. and we sat there for quite some time watching cars getting filled up, but my car was ignored. My black friend knew something was up and told me to forget it, let's just go. I was too naïve and said no, I need gas and beeped my horn. No response, so I beeped my horn again. An attendant came to the window and looked at us, and said, "We are out of gas."

I pointed at the cars and said, "What do you mean you are out of gas, they are getting gas." My friend kept saying "Let's go, Lets go."

The attendant bent down stared inside and said, "As long as you got that nigger in the car, we don't have any gas" and walked away.

Now I was ticked off and I said, "He isn't going to get away with that" as I put my car in reverse and backed into the pyramid style stack of oil cans which sent them sprawling. My buddy yelled, "What are you doing, we are going to get shot. Get out of here."

I put my car in forward and plowed into the other stack of oil cans as we sped off. I can still see those cans rolling around the parking lot and out into the street. We did laugh about this later. I forgot that Richmond was the capital of the South during the Civil War, and this was a time of racial unrest. This was when I actually, became aware of racism, as I didn't see it in Vietnam. It was ugly and I certainly didn't appreciate it.

With about 30 days left in the Army, I was given orders to clear the post. This was a happy time as I found out I wouldn't have to serve four years in the national guard because I served in Vietnam. I was honorably discharged on December 15, 1967, exactly two years after entering on December 15,1965. I was finally a civilian and homeward bound.

CHAPTER TWENTY-FOUR

FIGHTING THE V.A.

Decades after Vietnam and fighting through the many medical issues I had, it was time to do a little searching to find out what the root cause might be. After returning to the work force, I noticed I struggled with remembering people's names. I worked with these guys for years, some I went to school with, yet their actual names would elude me at times.

I was the editor of the plant newsletter, "The Two & You" for almost eleven years, and this would require interviewing salaried and hourly employees. Having to find a way to remember their names without asking was difficult but needed, to avoid embarrassment. At times it was necessary and I would get that puzzled look as to why? I would quickly say "Your name just is eluding me right now."

Another annoying ailment I had was numbness and tingling of the fingers in both hands. I would have difficulty picking up small parts, especially when attempting to build prototypes. I would become a softball umpire later in life, and this numbness would prove to be annoying when trying to dress into umpire uniforms or write down line-up card changes during cold weather.

Many NFL football players were complaining about short term memory loss, headaches, or other ailments after they retired. Studies were conducted in the late 90's into the 21st century as to multiple concussions being the problem. This was something I became very interested in and began to conduct my own studies as it possibly pertained to me.

As stated in chapters three and eighteen in this book, I suffered two horrible concussions within six months of each other. The first was in AIT when I was assaulted and beaten up while in charge of a barrack's cleaning crew in late April of 1967. I was knocked out, hospitalized for several days with a broken nose and two black eyes.

The second concussion occurred in Vietnam in early September of 1967 and it was life threatening. As written about in chapter eighteen, a heavy hatch cover fell on my head as I was coming out of the engine room. I was transferred by ambulance from the LST beach to the hospital where I was hospitalized for several days. I was then given bed rest upon returning to the 1098th.

I needed to acquire my medical records from the Army so I sent the required paperwork to the records center located in St. Louis, Missouri around the year of 2005. After waiting for weeks, I received a reply that they could not be found.

Depression was setting in on me big time. Thoughts of suicide was on my mind. It was like demons attacking me sometimes. I actually attempted it twice in a car in the garage. I sat in my car with the garage door down but didn't start the car. I just sat there and contemplated the effect on my family and climbed out.

The idea of getting in the car and leaving the state suddenly entered my mind. I even planned it out; taking back roads, eluding any detection and sleeping in the car in remote places until I reached a southern or western destination. It would seem like I disappeared or was kidnapped.

I planned an attack on the VA. I was going to strap fake bombs on my body and walk in and take over a room with hostages. I would pick a room with blinds or curtains so I couldn't be shot by a sniper. I wanted to make a statement, not just for me but for all veterans who got no relief from the VA. I could make the national news and I could become a martyr for those veterans. It would be worth it. Everything seemed futile.

Years went by and then I decided it was time to contact a friend of mine, Mike Clark, who was a veteran's aide through the VFW. Mike attempted to get my medical records also and was unsuccessful. He did help me by saying if I had "buddy letters" confirming my hospitalizations or letters home these would be very helpful in proving my case. He filed a claim for me but said I needed more information or proof to substantiate my claim. Luckily my mother saved the letters I sent home and I found the necessary ones. I didn't contact my two buddies (McGill and Arnett) in Vietnam I still was in contact with. Perhaps out of frustration or some other reason, I just didn't follow through and do it.

It was now 2015, years later, my condition had gotten worse and after talking to a few good friends, family and McGill, I decided to attempt it again. I contacted a person at the VA and he tried twice to get my medical records to no avail. Then I received a letter from the Department of Veterans Affairs which made me especially angry.

The letter stated that they requested my Service Treatment Records on February 3, 2016 and again on April 8, 2016 and did not receive a response. The letter than stated, "We have determined that these records cannot be located and therefore are unavailable for review. All efforts to obtain the needed information have been exhausted, and based on these facts, we have determined that further attempts would be futile."

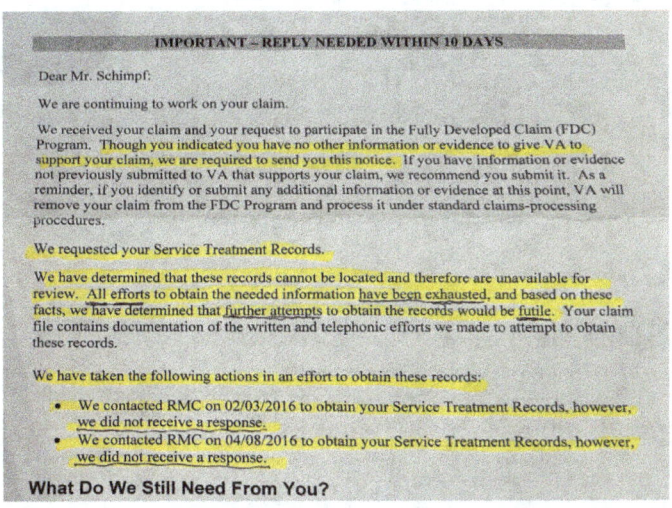

Photo of actual VA letter

This infuriated me! The VA was telling me to just give up. Giving up was not in my DNA, so now it was time for other measures. Someone told me I needed to contact my congressman, John Moolenaar. I drove to Midland to his office and spoke to one of his Aids in. They were very attentive and filed the necessary paperwork for my records.

One week later I received my complete Service Treatment Records in the mail! However, there was a very shocking result upon searching through them. There was no record or mention of either of my concussions, hospitalizations, or anything related to them! This was unreal. How could this be? I realize they weren't combat related, but they did happen. I now began to doubt the integrity of the military.

The only military medical document related to my injuries was a follow up exam which stated I had tingling of the fingers and hands. (see photo of that document below.)

Medical document

I again went to the Aleda Lutz VA in Saginaw, searching for an explanation. All I got was more BS and paperwork shoved at me. I had reached my boiling point and went off on the person at the desk in charge. I was now very emotional and in distress (I may add I had been under medication for depression for quite some time) and began to basically scream from about 30 feet away.

"You people don't want to help us veterans. You want us to either give up or Die!" I repeated this again.

Quickly two security guards appeared near the elevator and asked if I wanted to speak to a doctor or someone else. I said I didn't need a shrink nor any help. I was going to leave quietly and I got on the elevator and left. I was very shook up when I got home and told my wife, Linda, what had happened.

One of the papers I received was about an appeal process. I had three options. One was requesting a meeting with the local VA board, the second was to request a meeting with a higher VA appeal board and the third option was to hire a lawyer and file a legal appeal to an arbitrator or judge.

I certainly didn't trust any appeal to the VA so I decided to hire a lawyer. I began searching the Yellow Pages for VA type lawyers who handle disability claims. The Sam Bernstein firm is a large Michigan based firm who doesn't require any money unless they win. I called them and was referred to John Walus, an attorney from Dearborn, Michigan, about 2 hours away.

We had a consultation and he explained that it would be difficult to prove my case and even if I did, it wouldn't amount to any more than 10 to 20 percent or just a few hundred dollars a month. I said it wasn't the amount that bothered me now, but the idea of making the military and the VA realize how I feel screwed and wanting them to hear my story.

I provided John the necessary records I had, a buddy letter from McGill and my letters home to prove that this actually occurred. I also had some medical exams and tests (MRI's, Ultra-sounds, EKG's, etc.) which were conducted on me in the past year or two. I also had a letter of support from my family doctor stating that in her opinion the medical problem I had with my fingers and hands was chronic in nature due to an existing condition. This was also very helpful.

On April 10, 2019, I signed an agreement with the attorney stating his entire legal scope, his attorney fees (20%) upon final decision of granted disability back pay or retroactive award, and other pertinent information. He then filed a NOD (notice of disagreement) with the rejection of my disability claim. In my opinion this was the best decision I had made to resolve my issues.

The long process of proving my case had now begun! More tests required, specialized doctors, plus VA assigned persons like a massage therapist and even a TBI (Traumatic Brain Injury) doctor in Lansing. It got down to a ridiculous "cat and mouse" game of them trying to prove I wasn't disabled due to a previous military medical condition and me attempting to prove it was. He actually said, "they will send you to doctor and doctor and doctor again until you finally give up."

I was beginning to see the train at the end of the tunnel and it wasn't going to run me over. A neurologist determined that my condition was chronic in nature due to a preexisting condition due to a concussion. The spinal discs in my neck were compressed and deteriorating. Xrays, ultrasounds, MRI's were all substantiating this. It was now time for an impartial judge to determine my fate.

I received a letter from judge Sonnet Bush saying she would hear my case via a Zoom meeting (this was during Covid) on December 29, 2021. My attorney was present, and I presented all the facts and difficulties I endured. Judge Bush seemed very upset about the letter saying it was futile for me to pursue getting my medical records especially after acquiring them through my congressman. She had my records and noticed that there was no mention of either of my concussions which was very surprising. The judge listened intently to what facts I had was very sympathetic to my problems. She stated her judgment is final and not appealable.

She granted me 20% disability for my left extremity and 20% disability for my right extremity and then surprised me by granting an additional 10% for all of what I wasput through regarding lack of medical records for what was undeniably a previous condition caused by an accident in Vietnam. She also made it retroactive back to November 17, 2015, the date I first filed and was told it would be futile to attempt any more. This amount was over $70,000 before the attorney received his 20%. My 50% monthly disability check amounted to about $1,500.

BOARD OF VETERANS' APPEALS
FOR THE SECRETARY OF VETERANS AFFAIRS

IN THE APPEAL OF   SS 376 50 5278
DAVID G. SCHIMPF   Docket No. 191003-39242
Represented by   **Advanced on the Docket**
     John E. Walus, Attorney

DATE: November 30, 2021

ORDER

Entitlement to service connection for a cervical spine disability, to include cervical degenerative changes and cervical spondylosis, is granted.

Entitlement to secondary service connection for a neurological disability of the left upper extremity, to include cervical radiculopathy and tremor, is granted.

Entitlement to secondary service connection for a neurological disability of the right upper extremity, to include cervical radiculopathy and tremor, is granted.

FINDINGS OF FACT

1. The Veteran's cervical spine disability is proximately due to an injury in service.

2. The Veteran's left upper extremity neurological disability, to include cervical radiculopathy and tremor, is proximately due to a cervical spine disability.

3. The Veteran's right upper extremity neurological disability, to include cervical radiculopathy and tremor, is proximately due to a cervical spine disability.

Photos of Evidence and Determination

DAVID G. SCHIMPF   Docket No. 191003-39242
                         Advanced on the Docket

disability is related to the in-service hatch injury, it does not weigh for or against the issue of direct service connection for a cervical spine disability.

Here, the evidence of record shows that the Veteran's claimed symptoms are due to a cervical spine disability and related neurological disorders. All the probative evidence of record weighs in favor of the claim, as it shows that his symptoms are related to his cervical spine disability and that the cervical spine disability is in turn due to an injury in service. Accordingly, the appeal is granted.

S. BUSH
Veterans Law Judge
Board of Veterans' Appeals

Attorney for the Board   D.M. Badaczewski, Associate Counsel
The Board's decision in this case is binding only with respect to the instant matter decided. This decision is not precedential and does not establish VA policies or interpretations of general applicability: 38 C.F.R. § 20.1303.

Unfortunately my medical problems were not ending but just beginning. In early January of 2022 I began feeling very lethargic and needing naps regularly to get through the day. This went on for weeks and I thought I might have got COVID-19 and that was the reason. When it dragged into February, I determined it was time to go to the hospital.

On February 14, 2022 I was admitted into Covenant Hospital in Saginaw as doctors tried to diagnose my condition. I was scheduled to receive a heart pacemaker for a heart condition which occurred in 2021. This had to be delayed when it was found that I had multiple myeloma, which is one of the symptoms of Agent Orange. Once my immune system was strong enough, the pacemaker was placed in my upper chest.

In March of 2022, my left arm blew up like "Popeye" and I was admitted to the hospital again for 10 days due to a blood clot. A different blood thinner seemed to be a solution to this problem. My attorney, John Walus, said I needed to file for total disability due to Agent Orange. He filed the necessary paperwork.

I received a letter in July stating that I was granted 100% disability due to agent orange and multiple myeloma. I have been taking cancer treatment since March of 2022, although not the extensive chemo treatment. Miraculously I am now just taking chemo pills for 14 days and off for seven days, and repeating as this treatment seems to be working. Multiple myeloma is not curable but it is treatable.

My neuropathy has gotten a little worse. I now have tingling and numbness in the bottom of my feet. I usually can't feel hot nor cold on them. Of course my hands and fingers still tingle and shake most of the time. My memory loss when it comes to remembering names remains as well.

Believe me I would give all of my monetary award to be rid of my numbness, tremors, and this cancer. The whole purpose of this chapter is to let any veteran know to not give up in proving their case. I wonder how many veterans, do not have the proper medical records to prove a disability case. If this happened to you, please contact me. I don't have much faith in the VA. Determination and investigating is your best option. Don't give up. Keep the faith!

Left to Right: Myself, McGill, Campfield

SKETCHES BY MY GRANDSON
JOEY SCHIMPF

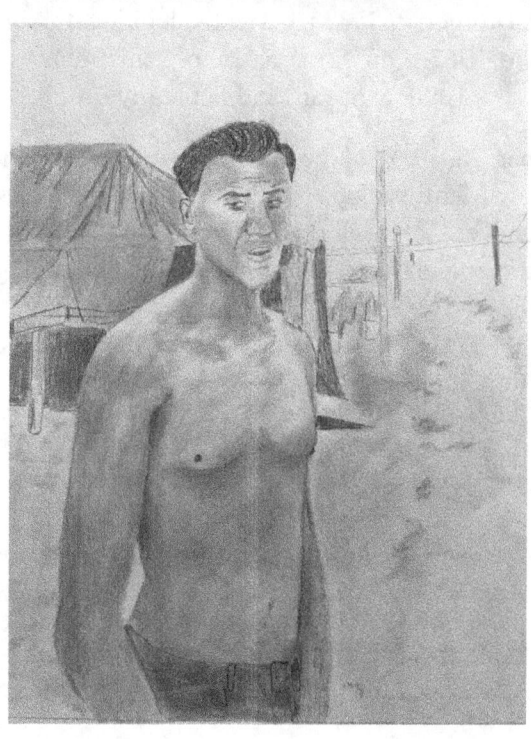

133

EPILOGUE

My story of just a plain soldier's tour of duty in the army and Vietnam is finally told. It actually took me five years to complete. I began writing this book on March 19, 1986, and worked on it off and on for four months before stopping on June 25, when I lost interest. It was over a year before I decided to get it done and restarted on July 1, 1988, but again lost interest in a few months as I had become an umpire a few years before and after work had little time to sit down and write. We also had two children, Joseph who was 15 and Angela, 13, who demanded my attention with after-school activities, which I loved doing.

During the fall of 1990 I began researching the Vietnam War. I would visit the library and check out any books of interest about the war, as I wanted to learn as much about it, because I basically ignored the war when I got out. I really wanted to forget it. I was basically looking for information about the years 1966 and 1967, Qui Nhon and more importantly, the 1098th. Any information about the 1098th was rare and not really useful.

On November 23, 1990, I began seriously writing the book towards completion. My own family didn't know I was doing this, as I would get on the computer whenever there was nobody around or I had real privacy. Finally, with just a couple chapters to go I told Linda what I was doing. She gave me a big hug and said I could get privacy whenever it was needed. I completed the book on April 21, 1991. I did it for personal satisfaction not to be published.

I decided in 1997 that I would like it published and wrote to a publishing company. I got all kinds of information on what to do and sent in my manuscript but the price of doing this was too expensive and I decided to forget it. When my grandson Joey started reading my book, in the spring of 2020, I again decided to check on a publisher. I found one who gave me what I needed, publicity, availability in bookstores, and the royalties were reasonable. Here it is.

If you are wondering what took so long, many veterans will tell you it's not easy to put into words a tour of duty during a war. It became much easier as time went on, especially the last year or so. What I remember also is that I never corresponded with Pollock or Collins who were still there. I never got their address and often wondered how they made out. I kept in touch with Hank Hoeffs for a few years, and then no responses back. I don't know what happened to him.

Les Cimino I would see occasionally when my wife and I went back to Baltimore, but after about 10 years, no correspondence again. Billy Campfield and Jimmy Johnson, I didn't stay in touch with either. Only Jerry Arnett and Bryson McGill have I stayed in touch with. We get together about every other year in Greensburg, Kentucky for Cow Days Festival during September. Those are great times. Both are drawing total disability from the Army for Agent Orange because they contracted sugar diabetes, which is a symptom. Jerry is now married to Lou Ellen and still lives in Grab, Kentucky. Mac is still married to Doris, and they have two daughters and grandchildren.

Linda and I have been married for 52 years, in reasonably good health, and our two children, Joe, still single, and Angela is married to Fred Matthis and living in Connecticut. We have three grandchildren, Joey Schimpf, Joe's son, living in Saginaw and Freddie and Eva Matthis. My mother died in 1983 as did my brother Don, and my father died in 1989. My sister is remarried and lives in Kalkaska, Michigan.

As for my reflections on Vietnam, at times it seems like just days ago, but mostly I realize it was over 50 years ago, and I don't know where that time went. The memories linger. The sights, sounds, and smell never really go away. It took almost 20 years before I was able to talk about Vietnam easily. I think about the 58,000 plus soldiers who never returned. Their names etched forever on the Wall in Washington, D.C. I have visited that wall several times and it is very emotional each time I do.

There were literally hundreds of thousands of physical and mental scars. Many lost arms and legs, or severely crippled and the thousands who suffer from PTSD (post-traumatic stress disorder) even today, and most of them were just teenagers.

How soldiers were treated back then was sickening. Those who did return were spit on and called "baby killers" by protesters. After spending a tour of duty in that God forsaken place, seeing horror after horror, seeing death all around and actually killing people, did the military prepare you for civilian life? You were on a jet going home, back to your "normal life", no counseling, nobody talked to you about how to prepare for civilian life again. Just go home, back to your families, back to your job, and just fit in. Soldiers would commit suicides, marriages broke up, jobs were lost, and many became homeless and still are.

These are the men who witnessed the worst and in one year had their lives changed forever. It took me almost 20 years to really get over it, and I saw little action. I still suffer with numbness of the hands and fingers and have been trying to get some disability since about 2005, when I realized that it was probably caused by the concussions I suffered in the army, especially the last one.

I found it hard to adjust at work. When I returned to my job in the factory, I was edgy, had a bad temper, and one time almost lost my job, just a year after returning. A guy in my department thought it was funny to keep turning the fan off that was cooling me off during the heat of the day. After many requests to leave it alone, I walked back to him with a large metal bar and said if he touched it again, I would kill him, and I meant it. It was reported to my foreman who chewed me out. A few days later I got into a fight with a guy and was suspended from work and almost lost my job.

Getting back into civilian life just was not easy. Looking back at it now, however, I wouldn't trade that experience for anything. The camaraderie, the forever friendships I made, the good and bad times, a person can never experience that again. I believe it's why many a soldier says he would return again if he could. I know I would. I would love to live just one more day over again. It would be neat to build a "hootch" in the back yard, get some of those guys together again and play some poker and tell tales. That would be the ultimate.

You had to be there to know what I'm talking about. I miss it terribly. But…. may there never ever be another Vietnam.